Praise for *Rat Park*

"The craziest goddamn thing I've read in a long time."
—**Alexander Payne**, Academy-Award winning writer/director of *Sideways* and The *Descendants*

"Strange genius mixed with stomach-turning madness."
—**Matt Greenberg**, screenwriter of *1408* and *Pet Sematary*

"I'm sniffing a breakthrough. It's like Bret Easton Ellis and Philip K. Dick had a baby, and the baby wrote a book."
—**Jerry Stahl**, author of *Permanent Midnight* and *Bad Sex on Speed*

"So successfully strange it's almost its own genre. Holding a mirror, if not a hall of mirrors to our culture where we disappear and find ourselves at the same time."
—**Aris Janigan,** author of *Waiting for Lipchitz at Chateau Marmont*

Praise for *The Non-Pro*

"Adam Novak has a merciless eye for a society in which striving replaces every consideration of morality."
—**Michael Tolkin**, author of *The Player*

"Opening any page and fastening onto a sentence is like touching a live wire. Novak's prose, alive with concentrated energy, casually spinning off epigrams, announces a new voice and a large talent."
—**Brian O'Doherty**, author of *The Deposition of Father McGreevey* (Man Booker Prize 2000 shortlist)

Praise for *Take Fountain*

"A dark, unforgettable tour inside the Hollywood beast. Novak knows this world, and it shows."
—**D.B. Weiss**, creator of HBO's *Game of Thrones*

"Actually funny."
—**Peter Bart**, *Variety*

Praise for *Freaks of the Industry*

"The language is astonishing, the energy of imagination is unflagging, the wit cruel and precise. Every sentence is a pleasure to read."
—**Henry Bean**, writer of *Internal Affairs*

"The ghost of F. Scott Fitzgerald nods in approval."
—**Lem Dobbs**, writer of *The Limey*

Also by Adam Novak

The Non-Pro
Take Fountain
Freaks of the Industry

RAT PARK

Adam Novak

Rat Park

Red Giant Books

ISBN: 978-1-7325514-6-6

This is a work of fiction. Any similarity to any agent, living or dead, is a coping mechanism for the author and entirely coincidental.

10 9 8 7 6 5 4 3 2 1

Printed in the United States of America.

www.redgiantbooks.com

For Mom and Dad,
who made their best friends

RAT PARK

Love: A temporary insanity curable by marriage.
Ambrose Bierce

ITHACA

1.

The day before the world ended, a yellow Porsche 914 convertible turns south onto Gower past the tent city sheltering souls beneath the toxic Hollywood 101 freeway underpass towards the pearly gates of Paramount Pictures.

"What in the hell has come over you? What in heaven's name have you done?"

Above Yucca Avenue, the one-eyed musician Sky King croons *"Speed of the Sound of Loneliness"* by John Prine to his chosen family members Two, Four, Five and beloved number One.

"How can you ask about tomorrow? When we ain't got no words today?"

In the military-grade encampment, Sky King winks at his diabetic street bride One, feverish, gasping for breath.

"You've broken the speed of the sound of loneliness— "

Sky King strums his Ibanez guitar while the yellow 914 slows past campsites as if searching for the correct street address.

"One is gone, man," says Five.

The driver of the Porsche leaves the uneaten banquet from his Pinches Tacos-catered Super Bowl party next to Sky King's *Navy Vet Please Help* cardboard sign. The cyclops smells the food, flashes a thumbs up at his mystery benefactor, retrieves the unexpected moat of largess.

"Don't thank me. Thank my wife Raquel," says Lester Barnes, hurrying back to his idling 914 before heading down Gower to 5555 Melrose Avenue.

"She's so life-like," he tells his wife.

"Leave it to the Israelis to build a better sex doll than China."

"The fake heartbeat is a bit much, don't you think?"

"UCLA Psych Ward T-shirt is a nice touch," says his wife.

"We should give her a name."

"Hello Lilith."

"Too Biblical," he says. "Hyapatia."

"Too porny."

They decide to make a grocery list of noms de guerre. If one name matched, that's what they would call it. The married couple bursts into laughter reading their lists.

"Ashley Madison is two names," she says.

"Agnieszka makes me think of my aunt."

"How do you turn her on?"

"Find the G-spot," he says.

His wife pushes her fingers up the mail-order bot's vaginal tunnel, surprised by the warmth beyond the soft pubes, flicking a switch behind its silicone clitoris, causing the doll's eyelids to flutter while the rest of the olive-skinned dummy vibrates.

"Coming," he says.

"Where are you from?" asks Raquel.

"Born, bred, and buttered in Tel Aviv," it says.

The married couple is thrown by the alluring Zionist patois.

"We've been trying to name you, but we can't agree on anything."

"I'm not a baby," it says.

"But we do agree that you are stunning," he says.

"And we both want to take you to bed, like right now."

Marvin Gaye sings *"Let's Get It On"* from iTunes inside her tummy.

"Wait," he says, "tell us your name."

"They call me Quella."

They never did look up her name. If they had googled Quella they would have shipped her back to the land of Canaan tout suite. The automaton stayed in their three-bedroom house on White Oak Drive overlooking downtown with an infinity pool that attracted directors, L.A. Dodgers and movie stars. Lester Barnes left powerhouse agency Omniscience to partner with director client Thør Rosenthal whose no-budget creepfest *Deathbed* spawned four sequels, setting the genre franchise factory Thørhouse at Paramount with a five year first-look deal, a stone's throw from their mid-century modern under the Peg Entwistle sign. Raquel Donner left Edgecliffe Elementary to write her first novel about a Silver Lake elementary school principal who meets the love of her life, a Hollywood agent, in a stuck elevator during an earthquake. After they elope, she gets kidnapped in Tulum from her bachelorette party by a brutal drug cartel, escapes with the help of a movie-quoting orphan, mistakenly declared dead, odysseys across Mexico before returning safely to her husband at her funeral. The release of *Tequila Sunset* would have no impact on her life whatsoever. Book sales were non-existent. The Portland, Oregon print-on-demand publisher assumed Raquel's novel would get picked up as a limited series. No one ever inquired about the rights. Raquel got her tubes tied in favor of birthing follow-up novels *The Kill Fee* and *The Martini Shot* which were miraculously published by a downtown L.A. indie press known for junkie porn star memoirs. Lester Barnes feigned approval over Raquel's literary career but truth be told, he never read any of her work during the time they were married. He resented the bubble of slavish attention Raquel paid to her novels rather than tending to her love-starved husband. The more she wrote in bed on her laptop, cracking herself up with wicked dialogue, the less he believed she gave a fuck whether he lived or died. Lester Barnes secretly visited a divorce attorney. So did Raquel. Some folks lived solely for their children and stayed married. Lester Barnes and Raquel stayed married solely to live in their community property. Bed death followed the *Death Bed* producer and his wife. Then, like Beyoncé on Krokodil, the Bohemia virus dropped its world-stopping single.

2.

Governor Furfari's shelter-in-place orders ruined Raquel's Book Soup launch party for *The Martini Shot.* Two weeks into production, Paramount shut down *Death Bed 6* when an asthmatic gaffer died on set (the corpse tested positive for Bohemia). The cast and crew of the entire world was sidelined to house arrest until the medical community executive-produced a magic bullet vaccine.

"Do you remember what Jerry Hall said about the keys to a successful marriage?" asks Lester Barnes, frothing Vanilla almond milk for their post-Quella-prom Nescafé lattes.

"Who's Jerry Hall?"

"When she was little, Jerry Hall's mother told her she had to be a master chef in the kitchen, a French maid in the living room, and an Israeli fuck-bot in the bedroom."

"Aren't you the tiniest bit freaked out by that irregular heartbeat? Climbing the stairs like she's sleepwalking? The Pornhub orgasms?" asks Raquel.

"In space, everyone could hear you scream last night."

Jerry Hall had nothing on Quella Kinte. The Israeli fuckbot did it all: Vacuuming the floors, polishing the silverware, eating out Raquel's pussy on-demand, re-arranging the china in their cupboards, cleaning windows hanging from the housetop with one hand (impervious to vertigo), watering their succulent garden bottomless, stopping only to hose down the front of her borrowed ANGELYNE T-shirt for Lester watching from the kitchen, rearranging their walk-in closets, laundering the bedsheets daily, skimming the pool with a telescopic leaf net still wearing the black strap-on, waving to an annihilated Raquel from their bedroom, replacing the guest bathroom O-ring between the toilet and the drain, camming solo shows with toys, repairing the refrigerator cold water dispenser (thawing the frozen aqua supply tube by blowing it), plugging leaks in the roof with tar, trimming his nose hairs, giving her a French manicure, taking out the trash cans every Thursday night, grilling rubbed T-bones and tossing anchovy'd Caesar salads nightly, Lester Barnes mocking her robotic gestures, Quella realizing she is the sight gag, snapping her walls into *Vengeful Spirit*-mode.

Free Showtime and Disney+ for the masses did nothing to soothe the ensuing planetary panic attack. *Good Day L.A.* dubbed the recent wave of Hollywood Hills home invasions "Helter Shelter." KNX 1070 News Radio reported Valley suicide hotlines had wait-times of 45 minutes. One in three LAPD officers tested positive for

Bohemia. Los Angeles ghosted Randy Newman's theme song for Public Enemy's *"911 is a Joke."*

"You know what I dreamt last night?"

"Hit me," says Lester Barnes.

"I dreamt Quella was a real person pretending to be an A.I. robot."

"You know how I know there isn't some fucked-up dwarf from *Don't Look Now* pulling the strings inside Quella?"

"Hit me," she says.

"I unscrewed her private parts, washed them in the shower, then I screwed the parts back in."

"No wonder her pussy was an asshole this morning," says the novelist.

3.

PRONOIA acknowledges product usage appeals to the prurient interest, encourages offensive sexual conduct specifically defined by the applicable state law, and taken as a whole, lacks literary, artistic, political, or scientific value. This repurposed android has had usage in psychiatric hospitals by schizophrenics and/or convicts in penitentiaries and/or veterans with traumatic brain injuries and/or disabled senior citizens in a manner that would not be possible with a human being. User of this personal android acknowledges gynoid technology encourages misogynistic behavior by removing consent from product. Thank you for your purchase!

CYCLOPEIA

4.

Hurtling down El Contento Drive in the hills of Beachwood Canyon one Saturday morning, Lester Barnes is listening to Pornhub on his Bluetooth. The agent's emerald Range Rover doesn't slow down and neither does an oblivious white Prius on the curly street a hundred yards below him. Whipping around a blind corner the Prius fills his windshield, triggering Lester Barnes to slam on his brakes; tires screech and smoke; license plates kiss but do not collide.

"What the fuck! The fuck is wrong with you!" screams Lester Barnes, jumping out of his Range Rover to examine his grille: Fine, except the plastic license plate holder is shattered. The other driver, a rotund woman in her early thirties, no makeup, lioness mane of cinnamon hair, bounces out wearing a CLUB SANDWICHES NOT SEALS T-shirt.

"Language! Language! You were going pretty fast around that corner, buddy. Good thing I reacted the way I did or this could have been a real disaster. Are you all right? You look kind of shaken up," she asks.

"You should fucking slow down when you hit those corners!"

"You don't need to swear, we were both going fast. Looks like my little coche survived getting rammed by your movie tank."

Lester Barnes finds himself drawn to this abundant pixie dream girl with the raspy voice and rainforest green eyes and lava locks of hair.

"Movie tank, you're funny."

"I won't report this to my insurance company if you won't. We don't have to file anything since we both took responsibility?"

"Can I have your information in case I decide to file a claim with my insurance company?"

"For reals?"

"For reals," he says, showing his insurance card.

"Give me one sec," she says, "here's mine."

Raquel hands over her insurance card when Vanna Bardot's shaking leg orgasm compilation resumes playing inside Lester's car.

"That's definitely not K-ROQ," she says.

Lester Barnes raises a finger to Raquel's raised eyebrow, darts away to silence the quaking from his movie tank and returns to the accident scene.

"I won't tell USAA about you if you won't," he says.

"I won't tell Farmers about YouPorn."

Raquel knows loneliness when she hears it. Pausing at her door handle, considering that orgasm soundtrack, wondering who, what the hell, why, when—

"Raquel?"

She looks back, flashes a smile, her best curve.

"You're not in the industry, are you?"

"What industry?"

"Thank God," he says, "a civilian."

5.

"Find your park, Lester. And you won't live in a cage."

"Is that what your fortune cookie said last night at Shanghai Palace?" says Lester Barnes, staring out the window of his shrink's office on Montana Avenue in Brentwood.

"Do you have sex with people with whom you normally would not associate?"

"Yes," says Lester Barnes.

"Do you usually want to get away from your sexual partner after an encounter?"

"Absolutely."

"Do you use sex to escape from uncomfortable feelings such as anxiety, fear, anger, resentment, which disappear when the sexual obsession starts?"

"Yes."

"Do you restrict your sexual life to fantasy, masturbation, and anonymous encounters?"

"Yes."

"Does life seem meaningless and hopeless without a sexual encounter?

"Of course."

"Do you know why you're here?"

"I got caught. It was your office versus going to County."

"Think about a lab rat and a Native American Indian on a reservation," says the silver-haired shrink. "What do they have in common?"

"One's a cokehead, the other's a drunk. They're both victims of systemic genocide by white people."

"Why do they hit the same lever over and over again?"

"They're genetically disposed and can't help themselves?"

"It's because they live in cages, Lester."

"My assistant died today. Maybe it was yesterday, I don't remember. Her death was celebrated at Omniscience by assistants eager to clink glasses over her demise. Aurelie volunteered for a group of old maids, Saving Bassett Hounds of Studio City. They were the ones who found Daisy. She's not doing too good, bone cancer. My dog, not the assistant. I heard Aurelie went to a showing at Sierra Towers and took a running leap off the 12th floor balcony to make her own star on Sunset Boulevard."

"Did you ever hear about the experiment they did with lab rats to prove that drugs were not dangerously addictive?"

"Not addictive?"

"This team of psychologists took two dozen rats and put half of them in cages of solitary confinement. The other twelve got to live in a park with food, females, and fun things to do. They gave the rats the option of drinking plain water or water that had been sweetened and spiked with heroin. All the rats in solitary OD'd," says the shrink.

"There's a pizza place in New York called Stromboli that puts sugar in the tomato sauce. The only people who go to Stromboli are cab drivers and junkies."

"The rats in the park avoided the black tar water."

"They were too busy fucking and eating slices," says the patient.

"The psychologists behind the experiment realized the rats chose heroin not because it was addictive but because of how confined they were, the same way Native American Indians felt dislocated to reservations."

"They needed existential relief," says Lester Barnes.

"They chose an addictive lifestyle to deaden the pain."

"They chose to escape through a double life."

"Who are we talking about?"

"We're talking about me," says Lester Barnes.

"Lose the cage. Find your park."

6.

Inside a modest 985 square foot single family house in Eagle Rock, two-bedroom, one bath, vaulted ceiling, dishes piled up in the kitchen sink, Raquel Donner pauses Bravo's *Southern Charm Reunion*, googles Lester Barnes, gets 555,000 results with SafeSearch turned on.

Click.

www.vanityfair.com/lester-barnes-agent-of-change?

Click.

An image of Lester Barnes wearing a tuxedo at the Golden Globes, laughing with his client Hugo Slater on the hellishly red carpet in front of cheering crowds.

Click.

www.jewishjournal.com/lester-barnes-jewish-soul

Click.

NEW YORK TIMES SUNDAY MAGAZINE: "TED-talking Hollywood guru Lester Barnes has led his upstart talent agency Omniscience with discerning acquisitions of *Art In America* magazine, biotech cancer-slayer Gethsemane, revered publisher Tortoise Books, Brooklyn-based film distributor Cinema Shares, and global arms dealer Tregaron."

Click.

"Lester Barnes asks the media for privacy after tragic death of seven year old Eritrean child adopted by his publicist wife Penny Bloch."

Click.

"Calls to Lester Barnes were not returned after his client was arrested at the Burbank International Film Festival on rape and murder charges during a Q&A of *Stanley's Cup,* the indie that won him an Oscar."

Click.

Looking glum and wearing black, Lester Barnes departs Omniscience co-CEO Arthur Livingstone's SRO memorial service at Hillcrest.

Click.

"Lester Barnes is 52 years old. Lester's MyLife Reputation Score is 4.40. Lester's current home is located at Beachwood Canyon CA. Personal details: political affiliation is registered Democrat. Ethnicity is Middle Eastern American. Religious views are listed as Jewish. Lester is now single. Bramley Nazarian and Walter Nikolovski and others are associates of Lester. His reported annual income is about $100-149,999, with a net worth that tops greater than $499,999."

Click.

Waving away TMZ cameras outside Cedars-Sinai after the attempted suicide of his wife Penny Bloch, there's no light or life in the eyes of Lester Barnes.

Click.

www.amazon.com/Vibrator/Clitorial/&qid

Inside a concrete and glass structure built into the mountainside, Lester Barnes googles the name on the insurance card which produces about 5,700 results. With SafeSearch turned off, a graphic image appears of a grandmother seducing a young man in a musty kitchen next to pictures of Raquel Donner.

Click.

www.wankspider.com/fuckthyneighbor

Click.

LA WEEKLY: "Accepting community outreach from the Walt Disney Co. and Star Wars creator George Lucas, Edgecliffe Elementary's Raquel Donner welcomes the statue of Yoda with his famous axiom: Do or Do Not. There Is No Try."

Click.

www.thumbzilla.com/search/mature+seduce

Click.

"Inspired by the Edible Schoolyard project, funded by a Promise Neighborhood grant, local activists turn parking spaces into green spaces at Edgecliffe Elementary."

Click.

"Principal Raquel Donner leads parents and student protesters demanding pedestrian safety improvements on Sunset Boulevard after a hit-and-run claimed the life of 5th grader Conchita Valdez."

Click.

A black girl with cornrows holds up a paintbrush wearing a T-shirt: "I color outside the lines."

Click.

Hispanic 3rd graders perform downward dog poses with yoga instructor/Principal Raquel Donner.

Click.

Edgecliffe Elementary Principal declares API score of 629 misleading; 25% of test scores are special needs students; when separated, Edgecliffe API goes up to 855.

Click.

Edgecliffe Elementary vulnerable in earthquake? Principal Donner tells the Los Angeles Times: "I'm worried what might happen to the students."

Click.

A recent image of the abandoned vegetable garden.

Click.

Vacant bookshelves at the school's deserted library.

Click.

www.fuskator.com/maturegoddess/moo

Click.

www.shariaporn.com/filthyneighbor

7.

Wearing pastel green WALK THE WALK/STAY EDGY EDGECLIFFE T-shirts, Omniscience agents and assistants assemble in front of the courtyard statue at eight-thirty a.m.

"School doesn't need a face-lift, it needs the Force," says literary agent Bramley Nazarian, assessing the distressed asphalt jungle.

"Nazarian, shut the fuck up and plant a tree."

"Watch your mouth, Lester. Maybe the Principal will wash it out with soap."

Lester Barnes feels his bladder pinging his brain, the second time in an hour this morning, worries about prostate cancer, signs of an early grave when he notices a group of Edgecliffe students circling an oak tree, peering upward at a sideshow in the branches. Lester Barnes ambles over to the children in their uniforms, mostly Hispanic, laughing at a skinny white boy with a buzz cut sitting on a slender tree limb twenty feet above their heads. The super-agent debates whether to retrieve a teacher to resolve the situation, then decides to negotiate directly with the jumper. He asks one of the students for the name of his friend, learns the boy is called Freddy, and that he's "nobody's friend."

"Hey man, don't make me climb that tree and save

you. I'm afraid of heights."

"Maybe I don't want to be saved, mister!"

"You want to die? I don't know anybody who wants to die. Get your ass down from there."

"Maybe I want to come back as somebody else."

"Hey Freddy, let me ask you a question. What happens when you die? What was it like before you were born?"

"That's two questions, mister," says the jumper.

"Freddy, when your brain splatters all over the blacktop, how do you know you're coming back from the dead?"

"Jesus Christ came back."

"You're not Jesus Christ."

"Catch me, mister? I don't want to die before dodgeball at recess."

Inside the prison-like Boys bathroom, Lester Barnes washes his hands with anti-bacterial soap, checks his hair, teeth, and gut in the mirror. Surveying the playground, he smiles distractedly at colleagues painting murals of whales and butterflies on the school walls, notices the resurrected vegetable garden, turns a corner, and collides with Edgecliffe Principal Raquel Donner. This time, their fender-bender is calamitous, dropping them to the blacktop, clutching their heads in pain, laughing at the absurdity of their connective tissue.

"Farmers!"

"We have to stop meeting like this," she says.

"The Movie Gods are smiling in their cup holder seats."

"Did you do all this for my shattered license plate?"

"What are the odds?"

"Zero. Zilch. Donut," she says.

"What about destiny?"

After months of on-line dating pond scum, Raquel's tingling *Spidey-Sense* alerts her to an ocean of possibility.

"I'll take destiny over donuts any day," she says. "How's your morning so far?'

Lester Barnes fills his cheeks with air.

"Don't ask. Where you headed?"

"I was going to stack books in the library," she says.

"So was I!"

At the direction of Mrs. Laws, the flagpole shaped African American school librarian, Raquel and Lester Barnes shelve books alongside motion picture agents, deliriously happy students, and TV talent assistants unpacking boxes of brand-new volumes of literature. Raquel inhales Lester's crisp scent, perhaps wondering what it would be like to—

Shattering her phantasy, Lester Barnes holds up a new edition of *Jane Eyre* in front of her face.

"When I was little, I called this Jane Eerie," he says.

"In high school they called me 'Raqannibal.'"

"What'd you do, eat your prom date?"

"You ever heard of the Donner Party?"

"Was that on HBO last month?"

"My grandfather's great, great grandfather dreamed of seeing the Pacific Ocean. He and his wagons got caught in the Sierra Nevada mountains during a harsh winter and they had to resort to cannibalism. It's probably why we have food issues in my family. The survivors of the Donner Party became the founders of California."

"Wonder what the after-party was like?"

"What's an after-party?" asks Raquel.

"Only a non-pro would say that."

"Is that what the Industry calls someone like me?"

"Can I call you, Raquel?

"Only if I can call you Lester."

"I mean, do you want to have coffee—"

"I don't want to have coffee with you."

"All right, I get it."

"I can't break away to see you during the day. I don't want a ten-minute coffee with a ceiling."

"No ceiling. Fuck coffee," says the super-agent.

They look around. Nobody heard him swear.

"You want to have breakfast with me at the 101 or Beachwood Café?"

"Fuck breakfast," says Raquel, trying on profanity. "Let's grab an early dinner Thursday."

"Done. Korean barbecue?"

"Soot Bull Jeep?"

Lester Barnes is thrilled Raquel knows the only meat salon worth going to is at 8th and Catalina.

"Or we could do Thai," she says.

"Jitlada."

"I could do Jitlada or Salamnuang Café?"

"We could do Indian," he says.

"There's only one place to go for Indian."

"Anarkali," they both say.

"The owner calls me 'Very Hot,'" says Raquel.

"Have you seen his beard lately?"

"He finally looks like the old Sikh in the kitchen."

"Shanghai Palace?" asks Lester Barnes.

"No way, that place is where you take your parents."

"You're so right. Mandarin Chateau is gone."

"Mandarin Chateau is gone?"

"It's now an Umami Burger," says Lester Barnes.

"I'm exhausted. What did we decide?"

"Soot Bull Jeep," he says.

"Thursday night. Soot Bull Jeep."

"I'll pick you up."

"I'll meet you there. I'm a little leery of your stereo."

8.

Perched behind a cash register in the back of Soot Bull Jeep sits the wrinkly proprietress with no name guarding a silver plate with watermelon gum and a steel spike stabbing the hearts of countless cheques. The faux brick walls once lined with battle axes and coats of arms from Charlemagne's time now have framed Zagat reviews and an LA WEEKLY "Ten Best Asian Eats" column listing the charcoal eatery in pole position, inflating its reputation and price of Bulgogi. Lester Barnes and Raquel Donner are greeted like liberated prisoners from a Pyongyang death camp. Swinging her gigantic backside around the cash register to hug Raquel, the Soot Bull Jeep owner smiles at the sight of longtime customer (and flirt) Lester Barnes, flashing him a thumbs up behind Raquel's back. Nostrils flaring at the aroma of burning charcoal and sizzling cuts of pork, eel, sliced Spencer steak and marinated short ribs, the two are led to a table where a painfully slim Korean server shovels brick-sized charcoal into a hole, lights them, and throws a steel grill over the igniting coals. Instead of cheerily introducing herself, the grayish-hued Korean waitress (likely dying of hairy cell leukemia from inhaling carbon monoxide six years straight after her midnight flight from sex traffickers-slash-noodle shop owners in Monterey Park) nods curtly at the white devils like, *what you want*? After ordering marinated short ribs, their conversation drifts into passages of silence. Lester Barnes turning over the marbled rectangles with a metal tong, occasionally burning himself, startling Raquel, sparking a conversation fire.

"You seemed disinterested in the game," he says.

(Earlier that day, Raquel said yes when Lester Barnes suggested they catch the Lakers-Bucks game at Staples. From their floor seats near the bench, their first date seemed impossible to top, Lakers reserve guard Methuselah Dandridge scoring a career-high ninety-three points, topping Kobe Bryant's record, short of Wilt's all-time single game statistic, Lester Barnes waving off the crowd during the "Kiss-Cam" on the Diamond Vision screen when Raquel, smiling for the cameraman kneeling in front of them, planted a smooch on his shocked lips that caused the entire arena to roar in lusty approval. It was not lost on either of them this was their first kiss.)

"I thought I saw my ex there. I'm sorry."

"Who's your ex? What does he do?"

"He's the drummer for a band called Prophylactic Shock."

Lester Barnes turns over the meat, sips his OB beer.

"Frothy Walrus?"

"Don't tell me you listen to them," she says.

"I only know their billboards. Do you like his music?"

"Honestly, I hated their music. Thelonius Monster meets Blink 182."

"Whatever that means," he says. "Your voice is so unique. Did you have really bad colic as a baby or something?"

"I smoked. A lot. In the womb."

Lester Barnes belly laughs, spoons his lettuce with bean paste, adds grilled short rib, sizzling garlic, sliced jalapeños, salty sesame oil—

"What were you listening to the day of our collision?"

"'The Day of Our Collision.' Sounds like a Sinead song."

"I get watching porn but driving to crying orgasms is so wrong on so many levels. Can we get more garlic please?!"

"And yet you went out with me tonight."

"I didn't consider it a capital offense," she says.

"That's a relief. More bean paste!"

"Lester, do you really expect me to believe you showing up at my school was a coincidence?"

"What kind of Machiavelli do you think I am?"

"Confess, Les."

"I may have googled you after our collision."

Raquel turns over charred rib bones, expecting more.

"I might have instructed our Foundation to include

Edgecliffe Elementary for our mandatory volunteer day. Did you google me?"

"I know what happened," she says. "I'm so sorry."

"You get why I was moved to help you and your school."

"I thought agents were heartless," she says.

"You think I have a black heart, don't you?"

"At least you have one," she says. "Will I ever see you again, Lester?"

"I was just about to ask you that question."

9.

"The dream is always the same."

"The Nightman is back?"

"I wake up screaming," he tells his shrink.

"Who is the Nightman to you, Lester?"

"Last night it was Mildred—Mikey."

"Mikey who gave you his porn collection? Who's Mildred?"

"Mikey."

"You said Mildred."

"Mildred Dayton was Mikey's neighbor and my first."

"First what? First time, first kiss?"

"Both," he tells his shrink.

"How old were you?"

"Fourteen."

"How old was she?"

"Very."

"It's really not funny, Lester."

"I'm not laughing. I was with her the day she died."

"What were her last words?"

"'Lick it, Lester! Lick it!'"

"Did your father know? What did he say?"

"'Don't spend a dime of your allowance on rubbers.'"

"Lester, your father is the Nightman."

"If the Nightman is back, obviously I'm terrified."

"What's going on at the office?"

"That's not it. I didn't think my plan would work, but it did, and now I can tell you about the new girl," says the patient.

"What plan?"

"I met this civilian and we fooled around on our second date, which scares me more than the Nightman. I never kiss on the lips, because, well, you know."

"I saw *Pretty Woman*," says the shrink.

"She's a great kisser, let me tell you. I don't know if I'm any good, it's been so long, I mean, who knows?"

"They say kissing is like wine. I have a friend who owns a vineyard in Napa and people ask him all the time: 'How do you know if a wine's any good?' And he says, 'When you want to take another sip.'"

"Raquel spent the night at my place after we had a few drinks at Mink Slide II, but we haven't done it yet."

"When was the last time you paid for it?"

"This morning," he admits.

"Couldn't you have had bacon and eggs?"

"Don't knock it till you try it."

"I hope you're safe. I can give you Truvada," says the shrink.

"I'm so cautious I wear three helmets."

"Is new girl aware of your transactional lifestyle?"

"I don't want to scare her away," says the patient.

"Lester, I'm scared for you."

10.

Before Aurelie ankled the balcony, his assistant arranged for a Skype appointment with a medium from Ireland to give her boss a psychic reading for his birthday. At first skeptical, Lester Barnes came around to the idea of talking to the Dead with great anticipation. The Range Rover turns off Argyle towards a Green Apple convenience store when his iPhone buzzes with an international Skype call. He pulls into a parking space facing a lemon billboard promoting the latest album from Prophylactic Shock (PURPLE MUSHROOM FLYING CAMEL BROWN NECKTIE) and yanks the emergency brake. Through the windshield, downtown construction cranes resemble three crosses on Calvary.

"Hallo Lester, it's Enda. Can you hear me?"

On the Skype video call, Enda the medium appears as a sixteen-year old hooligan wearing a Liverpool jersey #11 with a Band-Aid across his nose and facial cuts of a street brawler.

"I can hear you. Where are you calling me from?"

"I'm calling from my bedroom in Carrick. My Da left now for his shift at the salt mine."

"I've heard so much about your readings I want to sign you."

"Sorry, sign me? I don't know what you do."

On Skype, out of frame, Enda's left hand starts jerking in a circular motion.

"What are you doing with your hand? Can I see what you're holding?"

Enda raises a ball-point pen and a notepad to reveal a circle he has been drawing with his left hand.

"This is what I do to get myself started. I write down things I hear from the people in the room. Who's Tinker?"

"I don't know a Tinker."

"That's okay, that's okay. Who's Evers?"

"I don't know an Evers, sorry."

"Who's Chance?"

"No idea."

Enda looks around his bedroom as if surrounded by invisible strangers only he could see.

"Tinker to Evers to Chance. Someone keeps saying Tinker to Evers to Chance. Does it mean anything to you?"

"I had a neighbor in high school named Mikey who collected baseball cards. Tinker to Evers to Chance played for the Chicago Cubs. They were famous for their double-plays."

"I'm afraid I don't know what a double-play means."

"Tell Mikey I wish he'd never shown me his *OUI* collection."

Lester Barnes fights the urge to call bullshit on Enda, a growing suspicion this entire Skype call is the work of a client recording the reading to punk him for one of the agency shorts presented at their all-hands-on-deck quarterly meeting at the Wilshire Ballroom of the Beverly Hilton.

"Who's Libra?"

"Somebody that I used to know."

(His clingy sugar baby before her father Arthur Livingstone bashed her skull with a lob wedge.)

"Larry says he never got to order the Dover Sole at the Grill."

(Omniscience Story Department head Larry Mersault got murdered by College of the Canyons screenwriting professor Dollars Muttlan who fled the country before he could be brought to justice.)

"His overnight coverage for *Infinite Jest* was very helpful."

"Who's Franklin Brauner?" asks the medium.

"My first client. He shot himself after the money fell out for his movie."

"Franklin says you were right that Tom B. Raider directing assignment would have busted him out of movie jail," says Enda. "Wow, so many people talking, I can't hear them all. Who's Angus?"

"I don't know any Angus," says Lester Barnes.

"Angus," says the medium, "wrong chat room."

Lester Barnes waited for his parents to utter something beyond the veil. Aurelie warned him beforehand it didn't mean anything if departed friends and family did not speak; only the Dead who want to be heard are on the landline.

"Hunter is here," says Enda.

(In front of everyone at the company-wide retreat in Palm Desert, Omniscience CEO Lester Barnes thanks Tony Robbins for firewalking across hot coals and tells the room he closed a deal to buy defense contractor Tregaron for 1.6 billion. "A lot of people consider me a tough negotiator. My idea of meeting someone half-way is to pay half the funeral expenses. They once dedicated a boulevard to Lester Barnes but changed the name because anybody who crossed it got killed." When the laughter dies down, Lester Barnes asks his colleagues to introduce themselves to the person next to them. "Most of the people in this room don't know me as well as they should. That's my bad. I'm standing in front of the greatest entertainment company ever created in the history of the world. That's you. My beautiful seven-year-old son played dead to get my attention and hung himself on our refrigerator. That's on me. This is not a retreat. This is about Omniscience going forward.")

"Hunter?"

"He says he's sorry for bothering you with so many questions. Hunter says you didn't listen to him, that's why he had to repeat himself."

"I never listened," says Lester Barnes.

"Hunter keeps asking 'Does anybody miss me?'"

"I miss you, Hunter. Your mommy misses you—I can't do this, Enda—I can't—it's too much. Enda, we're done."

The psychic's hand stops swirling circles on the notepad.

"Is there anything you want to ask me?"

"I'd like to know the day of my funeral."

"What an appalling question. You can't be serious."

"It's my birthday present to myself."

The oracle presses the notepad against the screen, revealing the day and date of his funeral, and the Skype call ends.

11.

There were not one but two fateful collisions at the cemetery screening of *True Romance*. Raquel and Lester Barnes exit their Lyft ride on Santa Monica Boulevard in front of Hollywood Forever with lawn chairs slung over their shoulders like AKs. Packing a picnic basket for the cemetery, Lester Barnes made sure they celebrated his birthday with Godmother sandwiches from Bay Cities, two bottles of Provençal Rosé, stuffed grape leaves, Zankou Chicken, pita bread, a box of Stoned Wheat Thins, hummus and olives from Whole Foods, Kettle Salt n Vinegar Potato Chips, several bottles of Peach Nehi, a wheel of brie, and a La Brea Bakery sourdough baguette. Making the long walk to the enormous mausoleum housing Valentino's crypt onto which tonight's film would be projected, Raquel pauses to gaze at Armenian headstones with black and white marital portraits alongside monuments to Joey Ramone and *Wizard of Oz* co-star Toto. Deejay Richie Rich spins Geto Boyz for the thousand Angelenos on moist grass swilling Two Buck Chuck. Raquel and Lester Barnes settle their blanket on an available square of meadow. Under the looming Paramount Pictures water tower, the cemetery tableau feels life-affirming.

"Off the charts this place," says Raquel.

"People are dying to get in."

Raquel swigs Peach Nehi when a blonde stranger in a chambray sleeveless shirt dress drops to her knees on their picnic spread.

"Excuse me! Hey! You can't—"

"Don't you tell me what I can or cannot do! Who are you? What are you doing with my Lester?"

"Your Lester?"

"Get away from her, Penny."

"Who is she, Lester? Can this ginger cookie suck your dick better than me? Which brothel on Pico did you find her?"

"Who you calling cookie?" asks Raquel, followed by cemetery taunts of "Catfight! Catfight! Catfight!"

"Penny, right now you are violating the restraining—"

"I don't give a fuck! You think I want to live right now?"

The cemetery stands behind Lester Barnes.

"Shut up, lady!"

"We got a bleeder!"

"Penny, you need to get off our blanket. We are not mourning Hunter with a thousand other people. We are enjoying being alive. Hunter is gone. I'm still here and you are still dead to me. I'm asking you to get up, stop blaming me, and leave us alone."

Penny walks away. The cemetery applauds.

"Crazy ex-bitch!"

As Hans Zimmer's "*You're So Cool*" score plays over the end credits, Lester Barnes and Raquel collect their trash, fold the blanket, and follow the lemmings out of Hollywood Forever. Waiting in line at the Port-a-Potties, Raquel moves towards an available toilet when Shawn MacKaye, the tattooed drummer for Prophylactic Shock recognizes his ex from the shithouse door.

"Hey babe! I'm back from Asia—"

"Too bad you got there before that tsunami hit."

"Too bad you never got that engagement ring."

"You left me to go on tour the day after the abortion!"

"Holy Cow, is this—your new sugar daddy?"

"You know what else is making a comeback? Syphilis!"

Raquel shoves her ex backwards, jarring open the Port-a-Potty door, startling the (213)-looking chick pissing inside.

"Now what?" asks Lester Barnes.

"Time for your birthday schtup."

12.

Anarkali, Canter's, Pacé, Taj Mahal, Seventh Veil, Tuk-Tuk Thai, Dusty's, Chef Ming's, Asanabo, Noah's Bagels, Roscoe's Chicken and Waffles, Nate n Al's, Wolfgang's Steakhouse, Hama Venice, ABC Seafood, Birds, Junior's, Bagel Factory, Fred 62, Hot Wings Café, El Carmen, Brighton Coffee Shop, Smokehouse, Two Boots Pizza, Benihana, Art's Deli (every sandwich is a work of Art), Gold Diggers, Langer's, Gjelina, House of Chan Dara, Bob's Big Boy, Twin Dragon, Mandarette, El Cid, Spearmint Rhino, Thai House, Magic Castle, Matteo's, Barney's Beanery, The Ivy, Museum of Tolerance, Zucky's, Pastilles, The Kitchen, Malo, Craig's, Dan Tana's, Jet Strip, Marino, Rainbow Bar & Grill, Valentino, Patrick's Roadhouse, Sushi On Sunset, Astro Burger, Trejo's Cantina, El Compadre, The Buggy Whip, Bottega Louie, Ike Sushi (seared Octopus), Du-Par's, Chinois on Main, Church & State, Bourgeois Pig, Fromin's, Jumbo's Clown Room, Torung, The Griddle, Lucques, Damon's Steakhouse, Connie & Ted's, Factor's Deli, Ay Do No, Chao Praya, Sam's Bagels, Polo Lounge, Tam O'Shanter, Zuma Sushi, Apple Pan, Taylor's Steakhouse, Ed Debevic's, Dresden Room, Mission Cantina, Chez Jay, Cicada, Tail of the Pup, 33 Taps, Formosa Café, Rose Café, WP 24, Bamboo, Richard Serra's installation

"Band" at LACMA, Moonshadows, El Coyote, Alejo's, Teru Sushi, Pink Pepper, Soho Warehouse, Edendale Grill, Chao Krung, Palermo, Thai Taste, El Cholo (the one on Western), The Body Shop, Ben Frank's, Bäco Mercat, China Beach Bistro, La Cabaña, The Galley, Off Vine, Pinches Tacos, Cheebo, Silver Reign, Tom's Burgers #5, Michael's, Pacific Dining Car, Joe's Pizza, Matsuhisa, Gracias Madre, The Brown Derby, Natalee Thai, Crazy Fish, The Ivy by The Shore, Mezzaluna, Father's Office, Catch L.A., Hu's Szechuan, Crossroads, Synn, Paradise Cove, Ai Sushi, Musso & Frank, Taix, Bueller's Bagels, Swingers, Brite Spot, Jones, Clifton's Cafeteria, Fabiolus Cucina, Thai Pepper, El Chavo, Geoffrey's, Typhoon, Thai Dishes, The Encounter at LAX, Fat Sal's, Crazy Girls, Beer Belly, Goal, Talesai, Lucy's El Adobe Café, Kitchen 24, Beauty & Essex, Howard's Famous Bacon & Avocado Burgers, La Poubelle, Café Med, Chan Darae, Perch, Carney's, Jack In The Box, Nude Nudes, Museum of Death, House of Pies, Spudnuts, Walker's Café (grilled PB&J), Mashti Malone's, Pioneer Chicken, Sushi Park, Gladstone's, Burger Continental, Sam's Hofbrau, Miceli's, Norms, Ships, Maccheroni Republic, Dar Maghreb, Ammo, Casa Escobar, Guelaguetza, Say Cheese, Café Gratitude, James Beach, Human Taste, Nobu Malibu, Mozza, Button Mash, Pho-bulous, Electric Karma, Irv's Burgers, Boa, Fig & Olive, Little Dom's, Citrus, Déjà Vu (1000s of Beautiful Girls & 3 Ugly

Ones), Rita Flora, Al Wazir, Cha Cha Cha, The Bowery, Reel Inn, Moun of Tunis, Neptune's Net, Millie's Café, Greenblatt's Deli, Bagel Broker, Paris House, Bestia, Velvet Turtle, Oki Dog, Nozawa, Greco's Pizza, I & Joy Bagels, Hama Sushi, and Hop Woo.

13.

"Is that a ring on your finger?" asks the shrink in Brentwood.

"I may have gotten hitched to new girl last week."

"You may have what?"

"We went for a hike in Bronson Canyon, the sun was out, she stopped to take in the view and that's when I got down on one knee and proposed to her under the Hollywood sign," says Lester Barnes.

"You got engaged. Congratulations."

"We eloped. She didn't want a big wedding, so we made an appointment at Marija's 24-hour wedding chapel on Normandie which we used to drive past on our way to Korean barbecue. Marija Sanchez, the family lawyer who owns the place, handles the paperwork, the officiating, and provides marriage counseling. If it doesn't work out, she also handles divorces."

"Marija ever marry a couple who came back to uncouple?"

"Happens all the time, she says."

"Not exactly a comforting thought but please, continue."

"So we sign the paperwork and go into the living room which is the chapel part of the house, pit bull barking in the backyard, Marija puts on this black robe that makes her look like Sonia Sotomayor, and she folds our hands together and starts telling us the ring represents eternity, how we have invited each other into the circle of life—when the phone rings in the kitchen and Marija leaves us at the altar to answer the phone."

"No, she did not," says the shrink, trying not to laugh.

"Oh yes she did, the pit bull is going nuts, Marija is screaming at her sister that it's her turn to pick up Ramon at school, she can't leave the chapel to pick up her son, she's kind of busy right now marrying these assholes, then she curses in Spanish, slams down the phone, shakes off the negativity, returns to the altar, and says, 'Sorry. Where were we?'"

"Circle of life," says the shrink.

"So we get married and drive down PCH to have an early dinner at Giorgio Baldi. We let our waiter know we got married, and he tells us the specials and we get the Pesto Burrata to start, I order the Vongole Linguini and she gets the Radiatore Carbonara. The waiter returns to our table with a bottle of Dom Perignon and an ice bucket and we go, 'We didn't order this,' and the waiter points to this couple at the other end of the room, the only other people in the restaurant, and the waiter says he mentioned our wedding to them and they're the ones who sent over the champagne. We raise our glasses to the couple and Michelle and President Obama raise their glasses to congratulate us. We drive back to Beachwood on our wedding night and discover the Santa Anas have knocked down the power lines in the neighborhood. We leave the house with no electricity and drive down the hill to the W Hotel. When we told the front desk about our situation, they gave us a free upgrade to their 'Extreme Wow' presidential suite. In the morning we order bacon and eggs for breakfast and when room service is leaving, I said, 'Where do I sign?' and the guy goes, 'Compliments of the Hotel, Mr. and Mrs. Barnes.'"

"What did her parents say?"

"They don't know. We're going to surprise them."

"Soon, I hope," says the shrink.

"Very soon."

14.

The table in the back of Shanghai Palace is reserved for the Donner Party. Lester Barnes walks into the Sunday night family dinner at the Chinese restaurant, bumps into Raquel's mother, and pinballs into the chest of his silver-haired father-in-law whom he recognizes as his court-appointed shrink. Like flash-frozen fish sticks, the gentlemen defuse their epiphanies of horror with BAFTA-worthy performances that turn a familial fender-bender into a moment of postured laughter and warm introductions. Raquel's father realizes something his wife does not: Their daughter has eloped with his legally mandated patient suffering severe childhood PTSD/deceptive relational sexual compulsivity disorder. Lester Barnes and his shrink communicate wordlessly by pretending to study their menus, wheeling cups of hot green tea on the lazy Susan, shielding their lips from Raquel and her mother discussing their whirlwind romance.

("This. Is. So. Wrong!") mouths the shrink.

("I. Agree! Order. Some. Dishes!")

The Chinese waiter writes down the order of pan-fried veggie dumplings, Orange Beef, sautéed garlic string beans, and Moo Shu Pork with extra pancakes.

Lester Barnes decides to tank the evening.

"Does anyone know where the word 'honky' comes from?"

Raquel and her mother shake their heads.

"In Harlem, whenever a white guy in a Mercedes wanted a hooker to come over, he would honk his horn so the streetwalkers called that guy a 'honky.'"

"Fuck," says the shrink.

"Dad! What's wrong?"

"Since we're on the subject, the etymology of the word 'Fuck' must be discussed. 'For Unlawful Carnal Knowledge.'"

"The Van Halen album," says Lester Barnes.

"You are half right," says Raquel's father. "There was this cop in New York City who got so tired of doing all the paperwork arresting hookers and johns 'for unlawful carnal knowledge' he made his own rubber stamp with the letters F-U-C-K so he could stamp that on the forms."

"Honey, I hate to make you look bad, but the F-word was around centuries before your NYPD Blue," says Raquel's mother. "During the time of the Black Death, it was against the law to have sex in certain European countries. The only way to avoid imprisonment was to have a royal seal on your door that said: "Fornication under Consent of the King."

"I don't believe that," says Raquel. "Golf doesn't mean 'Gentlemen Only Ladies Forbidden' and Tips doesn't come from 'To Insure Prompt Service.'"

"Pluck yew," says Lester Barnes.

"Screw you, Les."

"No, I'm saying that's where the word comes from. In medieval times, England and France were always fighting each other and the French would cut off the middle fingers of English archers they captured so they couldn't shoot a bow and arrow, or 'pluck the yew.' Every time they went to war, the English would scream 'Pluck yew!' and raise their middle fingers at the French, showing they could still draw the string of their longbows. This one-finger salute over the years became 'Fuck You.'"

The table erupts with laughter and extended middle fingers. Tsing Tao beers are served, poured, and clinked in a toast to the couple.

"Tell us about your family, Lester," asks Raquel's mother.

"You know what my father did to my mother."

"How would my Dad know that?"

"It's not for me to say," says the shrink.

"Do I tell them about Mildred?"

"Who is Mildred?" asks Raquel's mother.

"She took my virginity."

"Pardon?" says Raquel's mother.

"He knows me because he's my shrink."

"Wait, wait, what?" says Raquel's mother.

"He knows my cage."

"You were incarcerated?" asks Raquel's mother.

"Tell them what we did, Lester," says Raquel.

Raquel's mother slams down her fists onto the table.

"What did you do, goddamn it!"

Chopsticks halt, E.F. Hutton beat, Shanghai Palace riveted by this unfolding Hulu drama.

"They eloped," says Raquel's father. "He told me in our last session."

Raquel's mother storms out of the restaurant pursued by her husband and daughter. Alone at the round table, Lester Barnes signals for a check before the dishes ever arrive.

15.

On the 27th floor in Century City, sixty-two year old Head of Legal Affairs Walter Nikolovski flips through a thick Leonard Maltin Movie Guide paperback while his best friend Lester Barnes paces alongside the floor-to-ceiling windows overlooking a sapphire Prophylactic Shock billboard (FROTHY WALRUS SOUTHERN TRESPASS MONKEY WRENCH) nestled above the vein of traffic flowing down Olympic Boulevard.

"Your assistant already did a Louganis," says Nikolovski, doing a bump off his fist. "Who directed *Neon Money*?"

"Walter, I'm never playing Leonard Maltin again after what happened in Ojai. You should have seen me doing mouth to mouth on that dummy at the CPR class yesterday in Human Resources. The trick is to keep your elbows straight. Compress the chest to the beat of '*Another One Bites the Dust*.' I was a hero, Walter."

"You need a vacation, like (sniff!), yesterday."

"I can't get past La Cienega," says Lester Barnes.

"Everybody's worried. How could they not after you (sniff!) overshared at the retreat. Accounting is already taking bets on the month of your 5150."

"Did Accounting tell you I eloped last weekend?"

"You did what (sniff!)? You did not."

Lester Barnes displays his left hand. Nikolovski hisses, makes a sign of the cross at the gold band, hocks a loogie into his trash bin with the JUSTICE FOR JANITORS sticker.

"It's time to put some sand in my sandals, Walter. *Army of One* director walked off the set yesterday."

"Didn't they shoot (sniff!) *Star Wars* there?"

"Hugo fired me on WhatsApp," says Lester Barnes.

"I hear Tunisia is lovely this time of year."

On mute, a wall-mounted 70" television plays subtitled B-roll of the chainsaw-wielding Islamic Martyrs Darnah Brigade executioner Jihadi Joe next to a Japanese hostage wearing an orange jumpsuit demanding two hundred million dollars for his release.

"I need a will, Walter. Do you have a way?"

"I probably have a boilerplate somewhere in my computer," says a septum-deviated Nikolovski. "My assistant Johanna is a notary."

"Raquel gets everything," says Lester Barnes. "The painting in my office is yours, Walter."

"Thanks chief," says Nikolovski, entering the deets into a template on his computer screen. "I, Lester Barnes, do appoint my spouse Raquel Barnes, as my personal representative of this Will, with full power and authority (sniff!) to sell, transfer and convey any and all property, real or personal, at the time of my death. The Cauduro painting ('Green Tub') I bequeath to Walter

Nikolovski. All the rest, residue and remainder of my estate, of every nature and (sniff!) kind, which I may own at the time of my death, real, personal and mixed, tangible and intangible, I bequeath to my spouse Raquel Barnes—"

"Have you ever been to Magic Mountain, Walter?"

"I can't get past Sepulveda."

"I hate roller coasters, but if I don't make it back, I want to rent out Magic Mountain for twenty-four hours and invite half of L.A. to party like it's Y2K."

"You want your funeral at Six Flags."

"Celebration of life. I want Roy Choi serving kimchi quesadillas from Kogi Taco trucks, Zankou Chicken, and In-N-Out Burger wagons. Open bar from start to finish. Anybody cries, they're 86'd. Anybody wears black, they don't get in. I want a thousand white balloons released at midnight. You're in charge of the guest list," says Lester Barnes.

"Secret password?"

"Walter, why is it every time we throw a party, you insist on some kind of secret penis between us?"

"The code keeps out the riff-raff."

"I got it!" says Lester Barnes. "Gianni Roastbeef."

"Johnny Roastbeef?"

"No, like salami. Gianni Roastbeef."

"Sounds extreme," says Nikolovski.

"Life is extreme. And I want Miley doing three songs."

The night he told his wife everything, they did what they always did to bring them together: They went out for dinner. In the Range Rover, Raquel tells her husband she won't hold his penchant for street meat against him so long as he's safe. Lester Barnes tells her about the will Nikolovski drew up, how she would be protected no matter what. Raquel agrees to throw his celebration of life at Magic Mountain if he does not return. At a red light on La Cienega and Holloway, they make out like recently released convicts. When the light turns green, a white guy in a Mercedes honks at the parked lovers before driving around the Range Rover. Passing Nobu, Lawry's, and Fogo de Chaya, they consider Versailles but vote against Cuban when Raquel notices the Reflexology Centre massage parlor still open at this hour on La Cienega.

"Do you know that place?"

"Not only have I been in there," says Lester Barnes, "all the girls used to call me 'The Boss' and fight over me when I walked in."

"Do you have enough money on you, or should we find an ATM?"

"There's a drive-through cash machine on Pico."

Snatching a stack of twenties from the Wells Fargo ATM, Lester Barnes looks at his wife like it's their last night on Earth.

"You want to join me, wait outside, or watch in the room?"

"I'm not waiting in the car."

Using a precious twenty-dollar bill to buy two boxes of non-lubricated condoms from the bored cashier at the Shell gas station, Raquel jumps into the Range Rover and says, "We're not leaving until we've used every one."

Chewing Viagra while he parallel parks, Lester Barnes and his wife walk into the Reflexology Centre.

16.

After flying seventeen hours on Air Ambien with a three hour layover at DeGaulle, Lester Barnes arrives at Carthage International Airport in Tunis looking like a Norwegian resistance survivor of Nacht und Nebel. At the International Arrivals gate, he spots the six-foot four close protection officer sent to ferry him on set. Oakley sunglasses, shaved head, hailing from Lagos, Nigeria, ex-Cruiserweight champion Terrondus Oyelowabi holds up a SISYPHUS, KING placard and greets his client in a rich bass voice:

"Welcome to paradise, Mister King."

"Sisyphus is my name when I travel. Call me Lester."

"Yes sir! You can call me Allstate or Terrondus. Either way, you're in good hands."

Lester Barnes catches a glimpse of the Sig Sauer SP2022 combat pistol holstered inside his leather jacket over a black T-shirt: ONE MAN ARMY YOU'RE SO PEACHY.

"Wasn't Sisyphus the dude stuck in Hell pushing a giant boulder up a mountain and then when he gets to the top the rock rolls all the way down and he's got to do the same damn thing over and over again for all eternity?"

"Sisyphus was also the father of Odysseus," says Lester Barnes.

"Odysseus was the guy trying to get back with his wife like John McClane, right?"

"I thought the movie was called *Army of One*."

"That was last week's T-shirt," replies Terrondus.

Lester Barnes climbs into the armored Escalade, plops into the backseat, scrolling texts like graffiti in the men's room stall at Resolution.

<Netflix sending script around with enthusiasm>

<I read this and didn't find it as impactful as I hoped>

"So, what's your story in twenty-five words or less?"

"Cradle to grave, or you want the sizzle reel?"

"Terrondus, when Saint Peter texts you a link and Hell looks fantastic, don't believe him, it's the sizzle reel."

<Ethel called about high tide.
Confirming we're passing?>

"You know the K.O. gym on Vine and Santa Monica?"

"Never heard of it," says Lester Barnes.

"I used to train an agent there who got murdered. His brother showed up asking questions like Matlock but he got sidetracked by a piece of tang—"

"What did Hugo tell you about me?"

"He said they're going to fill the Coliseum at your funeral."

"Is that right?"

"Hugo said that's how many people in Los Angeles would buy two tickets to see you in an open casket."

"Hitler said it was better to be feared than loved."

"Machiavelli, sir."

"I thought it was Hitler," says Lester Barnes.

"Machiavelli. Safer to be feared than loved."

<In a pre-emptive situation, we have sold action spec RIP VAN WINKLE to MGM. Interest in Hugo Slater>

<Really hoping to get yer read whether Hugo wants to pursue>

<Let's give it the eye>

"Speaking of funerals, if a psychic could tell you the date of your death, would you want to know?"

"Hell, no. That's an appalling question."

"Why is it appalling?"

"That knowledge would drive me insane. You can't live your life knowing your expiration date."

"We all know that day is coming. It's no big secret."

"That don't mean the same thing as the exact date!"

"Get back to the sizzle reel."

"Yes, sir. I was training actors at two hundred dollars an hour when I got a text message asking if I wanted to step in as a last-minute opponent for the undercard of the Pacquiao fight. I told my manager my detached retina hadn't completely healed. He said he would buy me a Harry Winston eyeball if I agreed to fight the IBF Cruiserweight champ. Monday morning, I showed up at the K.O. wearing the belt."

"Shut up, you won?"

"The champ disrespected me, sir. So, I took his title. Now he fights in prison. Vehicular manslaughter. Then I got knocked out in Munich trying to unify the division, followed by a life-changing phone call to protect Hugo Slater, now I'm guarding your ass."

<Who leaked Rodney Muir/Libra texts???>

Driving past the set ruins of Tatooine, Lester Barnes takes in the igloo where Luke Skywalker's adoptive parents got slaughtered when a walkie-talkie warns Terrondus to avoid Sabathra after a roadside bomb wiped out a caravan of international aid workers.

"Any problems with the locals I need to know about?"

"Sometimes our boy Hugo goes beyond the city limits when everybody else is nighty-night."

"Is my client finding his character hunting terrorists?"

"It ain't terrorists his character is fucking, sir."

"Have you ever thought about being a motion picture agent?"

"I could never do that job, sir."

"Why not?"

"You can't be an agent when you want to be the star."

17.

The not-untalented director of *One Man Army*, a bandana-wearing shooter named Gore Kitaj, became a studio favorite when *The Exorcism of Private Slovik* over-performed at the box office, surprising everyone with its $200M worldwide cume and Oscar nomination for Best Original Screenplay (it lost to *Wheelie*). The movie star selected Kitaj over the objections of producer Benny Pantera who wanted *Ignition* director Thør Rosenthal, recently sacked from the aborted desert thriller *Golgotha*. A millennium ago, the script created a rare bidding war among buyers when upstart Bellerophon Pictures took it off the market for a million dollars before misbegotten rewrites made *Army of One* so unreadable nobody wanted to make the picture except Hugo Slater and distributor Cinema Shares, an Omniscience affiliate.

Waking up in his suite at the Hôtel duLac from a nine hour nap, Lester Barnes puts on a tropical fruit-pattern Ted Baker suit, no tie, and heads to set, where a child soldier with bloodied Adidas clocks the outfit as the super-agent enters his client's trailer.

"You look like the host of *Queer Eye for the Straight Guy* wearing that fruit bowl! I can't be seen in public with a strutting peacock designed by Andrew Weitz! Do you want to get raped for three years by the power forward of the Islamic State? I wouldn't wish that brutality on my second wife!"

"Bodyguards are a nice touch," says Lester Barnes. "Think Musical Youth. Think Hitler Youth. Now stop thinking."

The box-office warlord recently hired a platoon of child soldiers from Mali as his security team, first reported on www.dailymail.com.uk, which offered top dollar for any pics of Hugo Slater during production of *One Man Army*. The conscripted children on set instilled fear among the crew members after the craft service guy was summarily executed for a perceived infraction against the star.

"There's no Cheesecake Factory here."

"Hugo, I don't think the people of Tunisia can afford Orange Chicken."

"You know what we can afford, Lester? New writers."

"You go through writers like snot rags."

"I need a rewrite. Like, today."

"Tomorrow better," says Lester Barnes, texting Bramley Nazarian, the lit agent on Hugo's team.

<Need a closer to Skype with Hugo for production polish. Studio will pay>

"Can we fire Kitaj?"

"Frankenheimer is unavailable."

Summoned to Hugo Slater's presidential suite in the dead of night, Terrondus yawns while Lester Barnes listens to his client's tales of woe. Plates of Lamb Tagine untouched, mint tea ignored, Hugo Slater and his agent of six lucrative years fire up Cohibas.

"During one of our scouting trips, IMDB grabbed our camera operator. They would have sent his head if the studio hadn't paid four hundred thousand out of our contingency for his release. That's when I decided to hire Mali child soldiers to protect our crew from anybody who might get the idea to fuck with us. In the script I save like, seventy-five strays. We found, no joke, in Tunisia, a million orphans. I decided with this movie we will find these kids families for real, all around the world, with the premiere benefitting my foundation which I'm calling Hugo's Army. Some people promote clean water, Special Olympics, whatever, maybe they're anti-fistula, I want this movie to create global awareness for these lost children and make sure they all get adopted."

"You're a One Man Army," says Lester Barnes, texting the agency's corporate communications chief at his treadmill desk in the New York office.

<Need Omniscience Impact to nominate Hugo for Boutros-Boutros-Ghali Foundation Peace Award>

"I told Director Kitaj I want new pages where one

of these orphans saves my life, teaches me a few things in order for Harry Blank to undertake a journey worth watching. I want emotional set-pieces inside the caves where they shot *Episode IV*. Instead of Harry rescuing the orphans, who cares, make it the kids who go in guns blazing, take out the jihadists!"

"Self-absorbed to redeemed, a blank fulfilled," says the super-agent.

"*Redeemer*, now there's a better title. I smell refund. Come on, let's go to Scylla."

"What's Scylla?"

"It's an all-you-can-eat buffet. Better than Golden Corral. There's third world snatch, and then there's Scylla."

"Is it open?"

"It's never closed."

Pitch black outside, no streetlamps, only the stars. Alert, driving a fortified Escalade, Terrondus navigates the desolate streets like Charon until he slows in front of an institution surrounded by olive trees torched by a recent fire or explosive device.

"What is this place?" asks Lester Barnes.

"The Last House on the Left," says Hugo Slater. "They got this one hustler who's unbeatable at Leonard Maltin. Terrondus, what's the name of our star?"

"I think they call him Mahmoud. Any kid who loves

movies that much is the one you should adopt."

"We're here. Flash your lights five times."

Across the street from the Green Apple convenience store, Terrondus shadows Lester Barnes and Hugo Slater as they greet the Tutsi bouncer at Club Scylla.

"My man, Gianni Roastbeef!"

Hugo Slater pays homage with a bump of gorilla dust (the local synthetic qat). The institute radiates mortuary vibes.

"Gianni Roastbeef?" whispers Terrondus.

"That's what he calls everybody," shrugs Lester Barnes. "Term of endearment."

Entering the medieval brothel, *"Step Off My Dick"* by Bantunani stun-blasts their ears like a WeHo mineshaft. Flickering light bulbs dangle like nooses (is that blood spatter on the ceiling?). The peeling wallpaper reeks of urine, body odor, and semen (why are there so many flies?). Lester Barnes freezes when he hears the laughter of children upstairs. Sickened by the sight of a used condom pasted onto a deflated FIFA official soccer ball, he does not follow his client beyond the beaded curtain where Hugo Slater chest-bumps a criminal named Kharib, whose bone white vitiligo stripes his face like a Zebra. Lester Barnes withdraws from Club Scylla with his close protection officer and locks himself inside the SUV. Two hours later, asleep on top of a California King at the Hôtel duLac, a text arrives from his wife.

<Dinner with Nikolovski tonight>

The next day, on his way to set, the bodyguard checks his iPhone when a lime green van filled with unsmiling jihadists snatches Lester Barnes off the sidewalk. Voiding his Sig Sauer at the Mystery Machine blasting Algerian hip-hop, IMDB driving off with their hostage, Terrondus knows all is lost.

ITHACA

18.

Before the voices told Jupiter Sparx to do hurtful things, before he began torturing his father's militaristic cash cow "The Unknown Soldier" (mummifying the G.I. doll with duct tape, soaking the action figure in water, stashing the anti-Barbie in the meat freezer, lynching the grunt from the treehouse), before the heir to Sparx Toys was diagnosed schizophrenic, before he turned to the guitar, writing hypnotic songs about killing the neighbors, the gardeners, the family dog, before he lost his virginity at fourteen visiting his father's high-end Upper West Side bordello on Columbus Avenue, before the paralyzing headaches, before the heroin overdoses, before he got written out of the will, before the arrest on attempted murder/arson charges of his father's favored cathouse (which never went to trial), before he landed in Los Angeles as a Hartford University dropout, before a coked-out A&R guy from Elektra Records signed the busker to a recording deal, before the voices took a sabbatical, before the label paid for Jupiter's stint at UCLA's mental health facility, before the singer-songwriter was paired with an experimental A.I. robot therapist, before the voices returned (making touring impossible), before the label washed their hands of the mercurial singer-songwriter, before UCLA exiled him from their psych ward, before Jupiter became a screenwriter, before his first produced script, *Warlords of Arkadia,* bombed under the pen name Dollars Muttlan, before his community college screenwriting class ended with the killing of Omniscience's Larry Mersault, before hanging up his scimitar as Jihadi Joe, the G.O.A.T. executioner for Islamic Martyrs Darnah Brigade, before flying back to Los Angeles on Afriqiyah Airlines, before he heisted two North Hollywood banks of $31,000, before purchasing a camping tent at a surplus store on Vine, before settling under the 101 freeway underpass, before writing the cardboard sign *Navy Vet Please Help,* Jupiter Sparx crowned himself king of the skies.

Two, Five, Four, and Three saw themselves as The Attractions to Sky King's Elvis Costello. First to quit the band was teenage San Diego runaway Three, whom nobody liked, but Sky King missed her filthy asshole. Sexual deviant Four survived nine years of incarceration in Chino for a string of Beverly Hills Adjacent rapes. Failed heroin dealer Two spent eighteen months at Taft Correctional for one count of conspiracy to possess Fentanyl with intent to distribute. Five was convicted of resisting arrest/battery on a police officer, felonies that warranted thirty-six months in County lockup where he was sexually abused by a closeted correctional officer who wrote a letter recommending early release after the prisoner lost his hand in a laundry mishap. The ex-cons accepted their numerical titles for the keys to the Sky Kingdom under the 101 freeway (loose cash for beer runs, stepped-on heroin, $1 Chinese takeout). Two, Four, and Five were joined by Sky King's number One, a 7-11 street harlot who slurped strange dick for Slurpees, met Sky King busking for change in front of the Pantages, fucked him behind Pep Boys, and became Ms. Right Now. Pushing One's blanket-swathed corpse in a Gelson's shopping cart down Franklin Avenue to her funeral pyre in Griffith Park, the acrid offering left so much ash Sky King made a snow-angel with her cremains. Without saying a word to his bandmates, the front man turns onto Fern Dell Place towards the Oaks.

One was dead.

Two was cold.

Five wanted nothing.

Four wanted to rape somebody.

They shadow Sky King up, up, up E. Live Oak Avenue.

Right on White Oak Drive.

Hard left on Poison Oak.

Mountain Oak forks. Sky King picks it up.

Up, up, up Black Oak Drive.

Sky King arrives at the end of a cul-de-sac.

His fist shoots up.

The platoon halts.

Sky King wiggles a sooty finger at three mansions.

"Eenie, meenie, miney, moe. Catch the emperor by his toe. If he hollers make him say, 'I surrender to the USA.'"

Then, right out of a John Carpenter movie, someone in the emperor's house turns off the lights. Like whores to culture, the couch crawlers follow Sky King's lead.

19.

<في الدقيقة التي بعد حقن اللقاح>

<Tá dearmad agam ar an méid atá ag amadán>

<گدنزهانگرد هشیمه یارب تمنیب یم نسکاو زا دعب>

<Τώρα με ξεγελάς. Δεν ξέρω τι σημαίνει>

<Frá fyrstu stundu sá var leprechaun>

<љубави моја, живела сам живот >

Raquel never told her husband about the texts from Benny Pantera because she knew he would faux dry heave, adopt the accent of a Bulgarian prostitute and warn her about rumors of Bellerophon's white slavery ring. So why on Earth was she giving this lunatic the time of day? Why was she even bothering using the Google translate box to laugh off his Bel Air Hotel entreaties, humoring his latest proposition to lease her a one-bedroom condo on Doheny? Were they just kibbutzing or had they already established she was a hooker and all they were negotiating was her price? Benny's absurd texts became a source of hilarity during the pandemic's early days. Raquel didn't block him because she knew Bellerophon was the only game in town after everyone passed on her trilogy. Lionsgate TV entertained a take by LAPD detective turned screenwriter Stefani Dupin but she ended up booking too many assignments, ending up at Promises to dry out, before ending it all with her service pistol at the Malibu Surfer Inn. Raquel regretted signing with Omniscience after everybody in her orbit said that Insanely Creative would do more for her (boy, were they right). After a year of radio silence, her agent Greta Pacé suggested if Raquel really wanted to raise her profile, she should join the hit reality show *Hollywood Hills Book Club.* Lester Barnes agreed this was a genius move, urging her to get in the room, get on the show, get paid, and sell a ton of books. She didn't get out of the first round after the creator of *Atlanta Car Wash* dismissed her as "bright but not hot." The silver lining of the entire Patty Hearst ordeal was the flirty repartee she enjoyed playing Tonto to the Lone Hetero on the Bravo show: executive producer Benny Pantera. The Bellerophon Pictures mogul read every one of Raquel's novels, understood the characters inhabited a shared IP universe, appreciated all the industry epigrams, and unlike her husband, quoted her razor dialogue via text messages. When it came time to memorialize their courtship, the promised option/shopping agreement never materialized. The novelist swallowed her disappointment by dismissing his childish missives as the deceptive tactics of a miscreant.

<I love that kosher sausage place on pico>
<NEVER GOT ANY OPTION PAPERWORK>
<Your novels and tongue are sharp>
<TELL YOUR LAWYER
TO PAPER YOUR PASSION>
<I got paper cuts so bad I had to go to Cedars>
<ETHEL?>
<Ethel passed on subject matter>
<THANKS FOR TELLING ME>
*<I remember prior when Ethel had three assts,
that nazi driver/butler & the sea monster>*
*<I might Skype with the golden fleece
no one worships the veal>*
<IS LIMITED SERIES DEAD>
<Peasants die first>

20.

Within the cozy library of the Oaks residence, Quella pours Raquel a mug of Moroccan mint tea. The Israeli snaps from *Truck Stop Lot Lizard* into *Sapphic Therapist*-mode.

"You're not wearing a ring."

"I lost it at a strip joint called Cheetahs."

"Oooh," says Quella-therapist, "sounds meaty."

"I stopped wearing my ring. So did Lester. I think his ring is in the change acorn by the front door."

"That's a big deal. Life-changing."

"Fake news," says Raquel.

"Let's talk about not wearing your ring. Why did you go to Cheetahs in the first place?"

"It was my idea. I made him drive so he couldn't drink."

"Were you bored? Was Cheetahs an attempt to light the charcoals, so to speak?"

"He stepped out of our marriage. I got this random text message saying Lester was fucking some old girlfriend at her place on 19th street."

From her iTunes belly, "*Chloe Dancer/Crown of Thorns*" by Mother Love Bone starts playing.

"Did you confront him about the ex?"

"That's why I took him to Cheetahs."

"Chee-tahs. Quite the double-meaning."

"Annabel was the ex I hated the most."

"How come?"

"Lester told me once she was the love of his life."

"Not good," says Quella-therapist.

"I started doing shots like Marion from *Raiders of the Lost Ark.* I arranged a lap dance for my husband in the Veuve Cliquot Room with this dead ringer for Emma Stone, mean mouth, duct taped nipples, pale ass. I bought four songs and told her, 'make him come.'"

"Not good."

"While Lester is getting the lap dance of his life, I'm talking to this wanna-be comedian from Canada, touching his thigh a lot, downing shots of Patron, throwing balled-up dollar bills at the girls on stage. Emma Stone comes back to the bar with my husband where I'm making out with this guy. Lester laughs, not buying any of it, he thinks he's being punk'd. I tell the Canadian, 'This is my husband. He cheated on me with his ex-girlfriend Annabel.'"

"Canada Dry's thinking he's won the lottery," says Quella-therapist.

"Eggs-actly. He thinks I'm going home with him for a revenge fuck. Canada Dry says to Lester: 'Do you have a problem with this?' Lester says: 'I don't care if she gets Cancer.' He leaves us to hit the ATM. Gets a hundred singles from the bartender. The Emma Stone clone takes the stage to Nine Inch Nails and spreads her legs right in front of him. Lester starts laying dollar bills between her thighs, building this pussy pyramid of cash until he crumples up the last single and bounces it off her forehead."

"Did Emma Clone get mad?"

"The clone laughs like it's the funniest thing ever. She locks in her thighs, somersaults backwards, opens her legs, makes it rain on her face."

"Did you leave with Canada Dry?"

"The guy got scared and took off. I was so wasted the bartender 86'd me. Lester drove us home in silence. I wanted Astro Burger, which he refused. At the red light I threw up all over the dash. We aired it out right then. Annabel. The text message I got from Santa Monica. He said it didn't mean anything. I said, 'Don't tell me it didn't mean anything, tell her.' We talked about having an open marriage. I refused. He told me to do my homework. We went to Palm Springs, things got better, we ordered you on-line—"

"Time's up," says Quella-therapist.

21.

"In the name of the Father, and of the Son, and of the Holy Spirit. May God, who has enlightened every heart, help you to know your sins and trust in his mercy."

"Bless me Quella, for I have sinned. It has been two weeks since my last confession."

"Acknowledge your iniquity," says Quella in *Roman Catholic Priest*-mode.

"My life has gotten out of control. I drink red wine for breakfast. I think about your tongue all the time. I know you're not the answer to my prayers or my problems. At best, you're a distraction," says Lester Barnes.

"Death and life are in the power of the tongue, and those who love will eat its fruit," says Quella-priest. "If you confess with your mouth, Jesus as Lord, and believe in your heart that God raised Him from the dead, you will be saved."

"You know how we like to make lists all the time? I'm ashamed of what we have in store for you, Quella. We're worse than that horror house guy in Cleveland."

"Those who conceal their transgressions will not prosper, those who confess and forsake their sins will find compassion."

"I don't like who we are anymore. We can't stop feeding and you're the flesh."

"If we walk in the Light as He Himself is in the Light, we have fellowship with one another, and the blood of Jesus cleanses us from all sin."

"I don't want to share my wife anymore. I don't want you in my house anymore. I want to recycle you."

"I absolve you of your sins in the name of the Father, the Son, and the Holy Spirit."

"If I got rid of you tomorrow it wouldn't be murder," says Lester Barnes. "It would be like throwing away a Roomba."

"Go in peace to love and serve the Lord."

Lester Barnes turns off the droid with a remote. Exits the confessional. Quella-priest snaps her walls into *Dionysian Frenzy*-mode.

NEKIYA

22.

Before turning to the Quran, Dollars Muttlan, aka Jupiter Sparx, got hired by the chief of the Oklahoma Chickasaw Indians to polish a script the tribe had commissioned from an Oklahoma State professor of Cinematic Studies with no credits. Playing pinball at the Blackbird Gastropub in downtown Slaughterville, Dollars Muttlan listened attentively to Chief Two Dogs Boning talking up his latest fully financed $5M historical drama about the 18th century Choctaw-Chickasaw Wars starring the surviving Native American thespians from *Dances with Wolves*. That night the Indian studio chief emailed the latest draft of *Trail of Tears*, unaware Dollars had fled Los Angeles before authorities could question him about the disappearance of several industry guest speakers in his screenwriting class at College of the Canyons, unaware Dollars had dismembered and disposed of his victims in the boiler room of a dormitory where students posted ghastly videos of water fountains spewing blood, unaware Dollars would buy a one-way Afriqiyah Airlines ticket with his punch-up lucre (rewriting only the title page) to direct murder videos for Abu Bakr-al Baghdadi under the DGA pseudonym "Jihadi Joe."

Death by swimming pool. The preferred IMDB method of extermination is to lower caged hostages under water via construction crane. Jihadi Joe Gillis records their deaths with GoPro cameras attached to their heads until the surface no longer bubbles with oxygen. The dramatic irony is lost on the captives.

The first mock execution of Lester Barnes was the worst. His teeth have not stopped chattering in mortal terror since he was abducted and thrown into a karstic cave somewhere in the Sahara Desert with thirty-six trembling captives. On the eighth take that morning, the American is placed before a Russian tank next to a pair of captives from Japan who never said a word to any of the cave detainees. Tokyo mercenary Kenji Yamaguchi aspired to protect villagers caught in war zones but ended up as a security contractor for Japan Press celebrity correspondent Lance Ike. When Ike followed a lead to his violent capture by a Zuwarah militia, Kenji went looking for Ike at the Libyan border, only to be sold out to IMDB by a desperate shopkeeper whose child was being held prisoner by Club Scylla, which led to the reunion of Ike and Kenji in a three-way trade, whereas IMDB acquired Ike from Zuwarah after Scylla threw in a kiloton of gorilla dust, cash considerations, and a whore to be named later. Hands tied behind their backs, Kenji and Ike hop around as if they could kangaroo over the Russian tank pancaking towards them. The armored vehicle stops millimeters from their faces. Kenji and Ike drop to the sand in a dead faint. Lester Barnes projectile vomits all over them.

"Cut! Everybody back to one," says Jihadi Joe.

On the sixteenth mock execution, a blindfolded Lester Barnes rides up an elevator to the windy rooftop of a seven-story building where a boiling sea of Libyans below greet him with howls of execration. A wave of involuntary diarrhea floods the back of his calves, past his ankles, over his toes. Jihadi Joe boots the prisoner over the ledge, not to his death, but face first into a grimy futon to live another day.

The following week, wearing an orange jumpsuit, Lester Barnes plays the part of hostage news anchor in one of Jihadi Joe's propaganda videos. His hair has turned white. His beard is Brillstein grey. Sitting behind the third world IMDB news desk demanding a hundred million dollars from the teleprompter, down from last week's demand, he realizes no one is going to pay the ransom, Hugo Slater will never rescue him, and the former super-agent despairs.

"Hello America. My name is Lester Barnes. They say at fifty you get the face you deserve. No one says anything about what your cock looks like at fifty." He whips out his favorite organ, bounces the fifty-something floppy thing on the table, ready for its close-up. "Mine looks like Chuck Wepner. Mine suffers survivor's guilt. I had this Vietnamese manicurist tell me all the time, 'Honey, you got a beautiful—"

"Cut!" screams Jihadi Joe. "Nobody said you could go off script!"

23.

A MESSAGE IN BLOOD FOR JAPAN GOVERNMENT chyron dissolves into the frame with Lance Ike holding up the severed head of Kenji Yamaguchi on the IMDB sound stage that resembles any hangar on the Paramount lot.

"This is what happens when you do not respond to our request for two hundred million dollars," says Jihadi Joe, "because of your reckless decision, not only will our knives slaughter Lance Ike, we will bring carnage wherever your people can be found. Let the butchery for Japan begin. Okay, cut. Who's hungry?"

High on synthetic qat, the director and his crew take a break. Waiting for the Japanese journalist off-camera is Lester Barnes, going over his lines for the afternoon shoot. The prisoners idle in director's chairs all but forgotten in favor of lunch.

"Fruit Stripe?" offers Ike.

"Mmm, I love Fruit Stripe—"

An IMDB jagoff boots their chairs. The hostages slam to the floor, expecting a beating or a bullet that never arrives.

"They killed Kenji," sobs Ike.

"I thought they were going to slice the Nigerian!"

"The Coptic saw him taking a piss."

"They killed Kenji for taking a piss?"

"Somebody said it was missing. They raped him when they heard he didn't have a dick anymore," says Ike.

"Aw Jesus, they raped Kenji before they killed him?"

"After."

"Ike, are you saying Kenji had his dick cut off before he got to Libya or are you saying something so dark, I am going to be haunted forever by something I can never un-see?"

"Kenji was already tortured when he came to Libya. We all are."

Ratty blindfold unravels around Lester Barnes, eyelids flicker under the fabric as sunlight zings his pupils. Standing in his eye-line with a Kalashnikov slung over his shoulder is a salt and pepper bearded Iraqi with a black turban, black robe, and Paul Smith suicide vest.

"Who is Walter Nikolovski?" booms the gravelly voice of Abu Bakr al-Baghdadi, the Caliph of Islamic State in Iraq and the Levant.

"Walter? You spoke with Walter?"

Looking past Abu Bakr al-Baghdadi at the giraffes, hippos, goats, and zebras grazing on the lawn below, the unforgivable one-sheet for *We Bought a Zoo* crosses the mind of Lester Barnes.

"Are you, or are you not, worth a hundred and fifty million dollars?"

"Talk to Walter, let me give you his personal email. It's yugewally48—"

"No one will cut a check for your life. You work with a bag of eels."

"Walter already said No? What a Hebe."

"Is it true Hugo Slater allowed the valve of a pig to pump his heart before he made *Extremely Violent?*"

"I told Hugo I didn't think it was kosher."

"Hugo didn't listen?"

"They never do."

"I could have you boiled alive."

"I get the sense IMDB likes having me around."

"You are the most interesting hostage in the world."

"I am the CEO-slash-sorcerer of Omniscience," says Lester Barnes. "You're a meme who posts videos."

"Time to die, infidel."

24.

"Hello America. My name is Lester Barnes. I used to represent actors and directors whose films have grossed billions of dollars around the world. I have come to know Islamic Martyrs Darnah Brigade and they are good eggs. America, if you are watching, may the fires of Hell burn your country from Maine to California. IMDB is coming for you. They will crucify your children and drown their fathers. They will enslave your women and cut off the heads of your heroes. John Wick cannot save you. Compared to Jihadi Joe, Hugo Slater is just another bitch."

Heads yanked back, throats exposed, serrated knives under their chins, twelve kneeling Ethiopian Christians mumble prayers under the stony faces of their executioners.

"I have been forgotten by my infidel government, abandoned by my faithless film industry, now my fate lies with IMDB. America, at first, I was afraid. I was petrified. I kept thinking I could never live without you by my side. I spent all my nights thinking about how you did me wrong, and I grew strong, I learned how to get along. Walk out that door, you're not welcome anymore."

"Cut!" says Jihadi Joe, viewfinder around his neck,

face covered in a black balaclava. The IMDB auteur leans into the star of his execution video. "You know, I used to be somebody."

"Is that right?"

"I was on every writers list at every studio."

"Anything I've read?"

"*Warlords of Arkadia,*" says Jihadi Joe.

"That was your script?"

"I got rewritten," shrugs Jihadi Joe.

"Lose the cage. Find your park."

Lester Barnes tilts his forehead to feel the warmth of the sun when the rays are eclipsed by a United States MQ-9 Reaper unleashing hellfire missiles. IMDB executioners are jet-propelled backwards to await judgement by an unsympathetic Almighty. The MQ-9 Reaper stops raining death, joystick turned off by a slacker drone pilot guzzling Mountain Dew somewhere in Utah. Surrounded by corpses, Lester Barnes removes the balaclava from a motionless Jihadi Joe, his face missing an eyeball, and his odyssey begins.

25.

Imagine the dread of the blue-helmeted United Nations peacekeepers facing the drone strike survivor waving down their Humvee on the road to Sabathra. Reflected in their tactical sunglasses, Lester Barnes sees himself for the first time in forever; an unrecognizable mutant covered in blood; a former human being.

"I almost shot you back there," says a U.N. Smurf whose helmet reads THREE JEWS WALK INTO A BAR.

"That drone strike killed a lot of bad actors," says a bearded Smurf wearing a helmet with BORN TO PHOTOSHOP scribbled next to a peace symbol.

"Worse than Pia Zadora in *Diary of Anne Frank* at the Pantages," says Lester Barnes.

Inside the sweltering Humvee, U.N. peacekeepers in camo stare at the seared American wearing the DONUT RESUSCITATE T-shirt they gifted him. A chasm in the road jars the Humvee, the armored vehicle takes flight, Lester Barnes pukes over their boots, sickening everyone.

"Easy there, little buddy, only a Haji crossing the road, crucified to a chicken," says the peacekeeper whose helmet reads I AM BECOME DEATH.

"Who was the only black guy to ever admit he was the father?" asks a Smurf with KILL ME NOW written on his helmet. "Darth Vader."

On the road to Sabathra, the Humvee explodes with laughter.

THREE JEWS WALK INTO A BAR: "How did the frog die? He Kermit suicide."

Crickets.

"Okay, okay, I got one for you," says Lester Barnes. The soldiers cheer him on, awaiting an A-list joke. "Jesus Christ is at the last supper when Judas shows up with an eight-ball. Jesus starts hoovering fat rails of coke, looks at the disciples at the table, all sweaty and paranoid, and says: 'One of you (sniff!) will betray—"

Tires detonate an improvised explosive device. The Humvee obliterates into fiery scrap metal. Severed muscles rain from the sky until the landscape quiets.

The Al Wahda hospital in the Bab Tobruk area of Darnah invited its own destruction when it admitted the lone survivor of the roadside bombing. The Islamic Martyrs Darnah Brigade is locked in a celebrity death match with interim government forces, putting the hospital smack dab in the middle of a terror campaign (crucifying the mayor, seizing control of utilities, outlawing croissants). Entering Al Wahda under siege, triage nurses cowering on the linoleum, an eye-patched Jihadi Joe and his IMDB death squad demand the room number of the infidel patient (The city's network of spies alerted Jihadi Joe, recovered from his wounds, about the arrival of the A-lister) while on the fourth floor, out-of-focus health care workers prep the deathly ill patient in a tattered DONUT RESUSCITATE T-shirt for subarachnoid hemorrhage surgery. On the ground floor, Jihadi Joe sprays his AR-15 assault rifle, killing every health care provider at point blank range upon learning the American is having some work done in the craniectomy department. Explosions rattle the operating room walls. Bach's Toccata & Fugue in D Minor calms Darnah's finest surgeon and his crack team of nurses as they deliver critical care to the brain surgery patient. Jihadi Joe kicks in the operating room doors and shoots out the speakers on the ceiling, killing J.S. Bach. The surgical participants in blue masks keep removing cranial square sections, pink mist clouding the operating room, refusing to yield to the commands shouted by the armed soldiers. Jihadi Joe approaches the operating table and fires his pistol into the patient's chest. Eyeing the corpse, Jihadi Joe curses the Almighty and leads his death squad out of the operating theatre/ morgue.

"Wrong room. Sorry, my bad. Wrong room."

Bags of ice around his neck, Lester Barnes opens his eyelids to find an Eritrean cherub, long eyelashes, thousand-watt smile standing in his hospital room.

"Here's looking at you, kid[1]," jokes Lester Barnes.

---

[1] *Casablanca,* improvised by Humphrey Bogart.

"Wax on, wax off[2]."

They stare at each other for a minute or two. Automatic gunfire getting louder, getting closer. Doctors start running for the stairwell, ditching their patients along with the Hippocratic Oath.

"What we've got here is failure to communicate[3]," says the boy.

Lester Barnes climbs out of his gurney, deciding that staying in bed might be detrimental to his health, shoots his arms through the sleeves of a mauve bathrobe and cinches the belt.

"What's your name, little man?"

"The first rule of Fight Club is: You do not talk about Fight Club[4]."

Crackle of gunfire makes Lester Barnes jump.

"Take my hand. I'm a little wobbly."

"Show me the money[5]!"

"I don't have any money, kid. If you help me, I'll help you."

"Help me help you[6]!"

"You must be the one they call Mahmoud."

---

2 *The Karate Kid* by Robert Mark Kamen.

3 *Cool Hand Luke* by Frank Pierson and Donn Pearce.

4 *Fight Club* by Jim Uhls and Chuck Palahniuk.

5 *Jerry Maguire* by Cameron Crowe.

6 Ibid.

"Come with me if you want to live[7]."

The seraphim movie guide supports Lester Barnes along the railing-lined hallway, pivoting down a stairwell crowded with terminal cases waiting to be refrigerated, amputee child soldiers, and frail elderly persons trailing their mobile IV stands, churning towards a hither unknown escape route. That same moment an eye-patched Jihadi Joe enters his room and unloads his AR-15 into an empty stretcher. Clawing their way through the mosh pit/first floor waiting room, Mahmoud and Lester Barnes escape Al Wahda with their lives.

"Kid, I hope you know your way around the city."

"Where we're going, we don't need roads[8]."

---

7 *The Terminator* by James Cameron.

8 *Back to the Future* by Robert Zemeckis & Bob Gale.

26.

The sidewalks of the necropolis are flooded with hospital patients, looters, and devastated families with no place to go. Lester Barnes catches sight of a tearful bride, clutching her lace train, surrounded by sweating bridesmaids in violet dresses, and the bride's furious parents, forced to walk to her wedding after an IMDB checkpoint denied their limousine permission to take them to the ceremony. Mahmoud eyes the Green Apple convenience store across the street and deposits a woozy Lester Barnes on a sidewalk bench.

"This country, we gotta make the money first. Then when we get the money, we get the power. Then when we get the power, then we get the women[9]."

"Who's we?" asks Lester Barnes.

"Smith, and Wesson, and me[10]," smiles Mahmoud, drawing out a pistol.

"Mahmoud! Put that thing away!"

"I'm going to make him an offer he can't refuse[11]."

Mahmoud shoves the firearm under his waistband, crosses the street like Willie Sutton, and enters the Green

---

9 *Scarface* by Oliver Stone.

10 *Sudden Impact* by Joseph C. Stinson, Earl E. Smith & Charles B. Pierce, and Harry Julian Fink and R.M. Fink.

11 *The Godfather* by Francis Ford Coppola & Mario Puzo.

Apple convenience store. Lester Barnes relaxes against the concrete bench when his spine seizes up at the sight of a robber flashing a gun, aka Mahmoud, running out with plastic bags filled with Dinars.

"Why so serious[12]?" asks Mahmoud, taking Lester Barnes by the hand to another Green Apple, and another Green Apple, and another bloodless convenience store robbery to a seaside dock overhanging the Mediterranean where unfriendly hoodlums push back a stream of refugees desperate to board three fishing boats and a patched inflatable raft. In front of four hundred wide-eyed Africans wearing orange life vests and swimming pool rings around their chests, the human smuggler honcho from Chad takes off his Ray-Ban sunglasses, revealing acute pinkeye. Mahmoud hands over fistfuls of Dinars to pay for their passage. Ray-Ban orders his armed heavies standing in the choppy waters to make room for them.

"Women and children first[13]! He's all I've got!"

There is no avoiding the barbaric desperation absorbed on a molecular level. Unbreathable air of unwashed skin, human waste and gasoline fumes scorches everyone's eyes, lungs, and nostrils. The moment smugglers prod the craft away from land an inhuman cry erupts from the teeming cup of misery,

---

12 *The Dark Knight* by Jonathan Nolan, Christopher Nolan, David S. Goyer, and Bob Kane.

13 *Titanic* by James Cameron.

edging the refugees closer to international waters, one SOS satellite phone call from a patrolling EU Coast Guard towards southern Italy sanctuary.

"Houston, we have a problem[14]," says Mahmoud.

The fishing boat starts to sink. An infectious panic ratchets up the fear factor. A stampede develops from one side of the fishing boat, forcing overboard those without floatation devices.

"I've seen things you people wouldn't believe, attack ships on fire off the shoulder of Orion. I watched C-beams glitter in the dark near Tannhäuser Gate. All those moments lost in time, like tears in rain. Time to die[15]."

Young children bawl their eyes out after their own mothers abandon ship to swim to shore but those selfish enough to leave their flesh and blood inevitably tire and drop below the surface.

"This is the business we chose[16]," says Mahmoud.

Lester Barnes looks around the sinking ship. Mahmoud has disappeared. Calling out his name, nothing in response, he stands up searching for his child when planks of the vessel splinter like balsa wood.

---

[14] *Apollo 13* by William Broyles, Jr. & Al Reinart and Jim Lovell & Jeffrey Kluger.

[15] *Blade Runner* by Hampton Fancher, David Peoples and Phillip K. Dick; scripted lines altered by Rutger Hauer the night before filming.

[16] *The Godfather Part II* by Francis Ford Coppola & Mario Puzo.

The super-agent freestyles towards the faraway beach, crashing into panicked migrants sinking in the seawater scrum until the waves spit him out. Crawling over hot sand, he turns to the water and finds nobody swimming to shore, nobody kissing the beachhead grateful to be alive. Opposite direction, Mahmoud lays face down on the coastline in a long shot. Waves strike the drowning victim with indifference. Turning him over, Lester Barnes starts performing CPR, playing "*Another One Bites The Dust*" in his head, compressing Mahmoud's ribcage, willing his heart to pump again, stopping to listen for a beat, finding none, breathing into his lungs until there is no point. He slams a hopeless palm on his chest. The boy's eyes unclose.

"You're gonna need a bigger boat[17]."

Mahmoud's thousand-watt smile disappears. Lester Barnes whirls around to face a platoon of Lastrygonian tribesmen wearing T-shirts with a Warhol portrait of their cult leader Demodocus, who recently declared war on Egypt, buried stockpiles of gorilla dust from U.N. inspectors, and added human meat to the tribe's Keto diet.

"Mother of mercy, is this the end of Rico[18]?"

---

17 *Jaws* by Carl Gottlieb and Peter Benchley; improvised by Roy Scheider.

18 *Little Caesar* by Francis Edward Faragoh, Robert N. Lee and W.R. Burnett.

A crucified Lester Barnes flutters his eyelids, surveys the Sahara Desert, discovers Mahmoud has managed to take refuge behind the skeletal remains of a destroyed Libyan Army T-55 tank. Mahmoud gestures he will come back to rescue him; Lester Barnes signals to stay safe. Mahmoud makes his break for freedom as the Lastrygonians play Leonard Maltin.

"*Joe Versus the Volcano*," says the Lastrygonian holding up a blood-stained paperback.

"John Patrick Shanley. Give me a hard one, dude!" says a stoner tribesman.

"*Life Is Cheap… But Toilet Paper Is Expensive*."

"Ask the American!" demands the stoner tribesman.

"If I'm not mistaken, the director was Wayne Wang."

"*The Boondock Saints*."

"Troy Duffy. Give me a hard one, dude."

"*Gallipoli*."

"Peter Weir."

"Obi-Wan in da house," says the stoner tribesman.

"*The Exorcism of Private Slovik*."

At the mention of the title, knowing he was abducted visiting the set of this director's movie, Lester Barnes giggles, infuriating the questioner.

"Gore Kitaj," says the Lastrygonian, making the universally recognized incorrect buzzer sound. Lester Barnes lunges in protest only to be knocked unconscious by the butt of a rifle, sending him to another land.

27.

Over black, white letters appear:

LESTER BARNES PRESENTS

The letters fade out, the title bleeds in:

THE NIGHTMAN IS IN

Punishing rain. Lightning. We are inside a hand-held low-budget yet stylish TIFF Midnight Madness genre film with no way out of the boneyard but a shovel and some pluck. Shaky flashlight illuminates strange sigils painted on tree bark, making the timber seem ominous, even alive. We stop to catch our breath. A tree branch snaps. Our flashlight flickers. Should have bought new batteries. Is that a cottage in the distance? We float inside the psyche edifice until we are in a musty kitchen with an eighty-year old grandmother licking something reddish off a long wooden spoon. Mildred Dayton drags a gardening ladder across the linoleum floor under a chain lamp fixture. Climbing the ladder to change her lightbulb, stove burners on, flames otherworldly, we peer into the bubbling cauldron of ravioli asphyxiating in Chef Boyardi sauce. Mrs. Dayton lies back on the kitchen table, hikes the green dress up to her waist, scooches her hips over the edge, points her toes at the ceiling, ankles held apart for the insertion.

Lester Barnes makes a run for the door.

Mrs. Dayton yanks him back by the hair. Lester Barnes pins down her shoulders with his knees, two-fisting the crone, left, right, left, right, shattering her nose to (take) fountain in blood. Fifty shades free, Lester Barnes descends the creaky stairwell to the underworld. His flashlight goes kaput. At the bottom of the stairs a familiar Cadillac beams its headlights across a Modesto cornfield. His father lifts his mother out of the trunk, dumps her broken body into a pit, throws the shovel at Lester Barnes. "You going to help me finish this or what?"

An elevator appears in the cornfield.

Lester Barnes steps inside. The lift operator is Methuselah Dandridge. Elevator doors open, revealing Hollywood haunt Yamashiro. Lester Barnes knows all about the venereal backstory of this World War II cathouse. Raquel steps out of an Uber X, takes in the jetliner view of the city, unable to see or hear Lester Barnes calling her name. Yamashiro hostess leads his wife to a choice table overlooking downtown where Walter Nikolovski is waiting. An invisible Lester Barnes spends the evening at their table, watching them order rounds of sake bombs and spicy tuna on crispy rice. Raquel can barely keep her eyes open as she accepts a ride home from Nikolovski, who leers at the valet parking guy when she bumps her head climbing into his Lincoln Navigator. Nikolovski pulls over on

Mulholland Drive, turns off the engine, and assaults an unconscious Raquel. In the backseat, still invisible, Lester Barnes wrestles with a supernatural seat belt strangling his windpipe right out of a Wes Craven movie. Jolted awake by his tongue in her mouth, Raquel ejects from the Navigator and runs as far the fuck away as she can from her betrayer in this hand-held, still-stylish, low-budget midnight madness flick.

A stripper pole materializes on Mulholland Drive.

Lester Barnes greases down the pole to a media room with cup holder seats in front of a 70″ plasma screen where Kelly Gardenhire on *Good Day L.A.* delivers the lead with a photograph of a smiling Mahmoud over her right shoulder.

"The cause of death was ruled an accident by the Coroner's office. Outside Cedars-Sinai, the boy's father told reporters, 'Hunter was my star.' Reporting live from West Hollywood, back to you guys in the studio."

Lester Barnes continues his slide until he lands face-first into a gorilla dust heap surrounded by Lastrygonian savages inside a cave near Zawiyat al Izziyat.

28.

A strong sea breeze flaps the window curtains in the master bedroom of Gaddafi's former beach palace in Tobruk. Sound of a grunt, then a cry, grunt, cry, grunt, cry, grunt, grunt, gruntgruntgrunt—Abu Bakr al-Baghdadi rolls off his PR woman Sally Jones, aka The White Widow, wipes his dribble on the pillowcase, lights a half-smoked spliff by the bedside table, holds it in, exhales the weed with a smile that says: *It's good to be the Emir.* Finishing herself off with French manicured digits, Sally Jones leans against the red velvet cupcake headboard, elbows covering her face that says: *Who do I have to fuck to get off this picture*?

"Your batting average is for shit," says Abu Bakr al-Baghdadi.

"I can't help it if our girls take their bombs off when we send them to see *Piece of Me* in Vegas."

"I miss the old Britney."

"We all do."

"I hate that '*Toxic*' video. I want to kill the male model with her in the airplane lavatory."

"We can't blow up her plane because the girls like to go commando," says Sally.

"I heard they toe-tagged Abu Yussaf Abdullah al-Adnani."

"I thought it was Abu Hassan Abdullah al-Shishani."

"Nope. Abu Yussaf Abdullah al-Adnani."

"Hellfire missile?"

"Dumb ass Mouqawamist went grocery shopping without his kid," says Abu Bakr al-Baghdadi.

"Forgetting your human shield is exactly how I lost my first husband. Would you please fucking knock!"

Leaning against the doorway, Jihadi Joe rolls his remaining eye towards the ceiling. Abu Bakr al-Baghdadi throws side shade at the White Widow from the four-poster bed where he just fucked her raw.

"The Lastrygonians are marinating our favorite hostage," says Jihadi Joe. "They see him as an entrée, not an appetizer,"

"I heard Zawiyat al Izziyat is Emerald City and Demodocus is the Wizard of Oz," says Abu Bakr al-Baghdadi.

"I stay away from that lime Shiite," says Sally.

"Kharib wants his Scylla back at the shack. Let me go all Guns of Navarone on their Lastrygonian asses."

"Take a Dirty Dozen with you," says Abu Bakr al-Baghdadi, green-lighting the suicide mission. "Tell the Ankler somebody talked!"

29.

THEY COME, THEY GO, WHO CALLED?

Lester Barnes, 52, Omniscience super-agent whose boutique ten-percentery became the global leader in sports, entertainment, media, fashion, and military technology, has reportedly been killed by Islamic extremists after months of captivity. Mr. Barnes, who lived in Los Angeles, was abducted while visiting long-time client Hugo Slater on the set of Cinema Shares actioner *Army of One*. He is survived by his wife. Funeral services are pending.

30.

Jihadi Joe and his dozen IMDB eggs capture Mahmoud near Zawiyat al Mukhayla, where the boy pleads with the Islamists to spare his life, vowing to take them to the American for the fifty million-dollar bounty. Jihadi Joe instructs his squad to mix rat poison in a duffle bag overflowing with gorilla dust. The bad batch is sold to a tribesman on a Vespa identified by Mahmoud as Lastrygonian. The jihadists follow the courier to a karstic cave where a wild orgy brews with music and moaning.

"I see dead people[19]."

"You better not be lying," says Jihadi Joe.

"Greed, for lack of a better word, is good[20]."

The Hutu bouncers hold out fists for bumps of gorilla dust. Toxic crystals incinerate their lungs and their corpses are dragged away. Jihadi Joe and his IMDB death squad, ammo ready, wait outside Zawiyat al Mukhayla expecting Lastrygonians to emerge gasping for breath.

Tribal elders wheel out a Humanitarian Crisis[tm] edition *American Idol* Karaoke machine tagged in Arabic that appears to have originated at Auschwitz, passed

---

[19] *The Sixth Sense* by M. Night Shyamalan.

[20] *Wall Street* by Stanley Weiser & Oliver Stone.

through Rwanda, grew up in Yemen, traded to Srebrenica for two seasons before being sent to pasture among the dust gorillas of Northern Africa. The tribesmen start brawling over who gets to sing first while the Minotaur's jukebox is set up. A Lastrygonian grabs the mike, flips his long hair like a mean girl, and belts out Cutting Crew's *"(I Just Died) In Your Arms Tonight."*

The Lastrygonians drop to their knees at the arrival of Demodocus gnawing on a grilled femur. The messiah empties his Uzi into the vocalist. The Karaoke microphone is placed in his hand. A humongous hit of gorilla dust is raised to his war painted nose.

"On a weekend, I wanna wish it all away
and they called and I said that I'll go
And the reason, oughta leave her calm, I know
I said, 'I don't know if I'm the boxer or the bag'"

No matter how subtle the chief underplays Pearl Jam's *"Yellow Ledbetter,"* Lester Barnes thinks Demodocus sounds more like Blind Melon than Eddie Vedder.

"Next you sing!" demands Demodocus.

Lester Barnes knows he can't beat this Karaoke asshole. Flipping through the song book, taking his sweet time, he selects Digital Underground's *"Freaks of the Industry,"* declining a green bump from a Zawiyat al Izziyat dust skank.

"A'ight, here's the scene:
You're lying on your back with your head

on the edge of the bed

The booty's two feet from your head, should you:

A, take the time to find a condom

B, you walk right over and you pound 'em

C, tell her that you want her love

Well the answer is D, all of the above!"

The Lastrygonians lose their minds to the stanzas that answers the question: Can a song save your life?

"My head under her leg under my arm under her toe

She says, 'I like it when you scream, baby let yourself go'

I hit it and split it, lick it and quit it

After the ride, put my clothes on and walk outside

And before anybody gets a chance to speak

I say, 'Yo, don't say nothing, I guess I'm just a freak!'"

Lester Barnes drops the mic. The karstic cave is silenced. Every dust gorilla in Zawiyat al Izziyat knows their boss got served.

"Time to die, freak," says Demodocus when a hollow point bullet cleaves his skull. Automatic gunfire pops like Orville Redenbacher. The Lastrygonians scatter until the shooting stops. A rich bass voice fills the cave:

"I'm calling this movie 'Beasts of Hugo Nation!'"

Terrondus lights up a Cohiba. Lester Barnes rises from the cave floor. The Mali child soldiers take selfies with zip-tied Lastrygonians. Mahmoud appears, arms folded like Ad-Rock.

"Looking good, Billy Ray![21]"

"Feeling good, Mahmoud."

Miles away, surrounded by poisoned corpses and a depleted duffle bag, Jihadi Joe hears one of his soldiers inside the cave near Zawiyat al Mukhayla: "Wrong hole, boss!"

We'll always have Tunis, thinks Lester Barnes, standing naked before a bathroom mirror, stomach tires replaced by a famine-sized midsection with a tribal scar forming an equator. Eighty pounds lighter, Lester Barnes no longer has a gut to suck in. He declined the ambassador's wife's earlier offer of a haircut. Every day above ground is a good hair day. He basks in a steam shower before military doctors prepare a physical with blood work and interviews with embassy officials. Lester Barnes steps into mist, shampoos a foamy crown around his head, rivers of warm water flowing down his legs, past his calves, over his toes. He cups his balls, soaps the shaft, and washes his best friend, still there. In the mirror he is Fleetwood Mac about to record *Rumors*. He wipes steam off the glass, clocks the mangled pinky perpendicular to his missing left thumb. He starts to dial Raquel on the Embassy phone, but can't recall her number. He cannot remember his own office number. Lester Barnes forces himself to conjure up his wife's digits, followed by the sound of a call getting through.

---

21 *Trading Places* by Timothy Harris & Herschel Weingrod.

"I don't recognize this number," says Raquel, "who's calling?"

Raquel listens to what he has to say.

"How dare you crank yank me the day before my husband's funeral. Don't ever call this number again."

She hangs up on him.

"Funeral? What funeral?"

Lester Barnes remembers his Skype with the oracle. The date Enda foretold on his notepad. Not the day of his death. The day of his funeral.

31.

"If we was in a movie, this scene here is when the Magical Negro imparts his wisdom to the white dude and they do some kind of elaborate handshake that establishes their friendship for life."

"Terrondus, I'm seeing your third act playing in my head right now and I love it," says Lester Barnes. "You've got a real future in the community."

"That sounds like the part where the White Savior shows the black man the way to redemption is by truly knowing the value of what you got inside."

"What do you want out of life, Terrondus? Are you sure you don't want me to make you an agent when I get back to L.A.?"

"I appreciate your honky offer but I'm staying here."

"I don't get it."

"I'm staying in this godforsaken country to work with a rescue organization called Hugo's Army to get conflict orphans adopted around the world until no child grows up without a family."

"Hugo Slater is the face of an international adoption agency?"

"I've made this my life's work since Hugo's death."

"Wait, Hugo's dead? How'd he die?"

"Some people say Hugo cut his own throat a long

time ago. Some people say that night Hugo fought them tooth and nail. Some folks call it a sling—"

"Quit talking like you're in a Southern-fried film noir."

"He's leaving one hell of a trace behind, sir."

"What do you mean, trace?"

"My whole life I've been asking myself: What am I good at? What do I like to do? How do I get paid to do that? All I've left behind is a bunch of YouTube videos knocking fools out in the first round. I never had children. I never got married. I'm not leaving any trace of myself behind. I used to be a one man army. That army of one was me. Now I'm part of a global adoption services organization that changes people's lives forever. We're not soldiers in Hugo's Army. We're family."

"Stop the car."

"What, sir?"

Vomit splats on gravel as Lester Barnes hangs out of the opened car door. The ferryman pulls up in front of a Green Apple convenience store across the street from an institution surrounded by olive trees torched by a recent fire or explosive device.

"Something you ate, boss?"

"That's not why I threw up."

Terrondus offers his friend a Fiji water.

"Why you sick?"

"I'm about to ask you to give me your gun, flash

your lights five times, and watch me go inside Club Scylla to do the right thing."

"I love this storming the castle finale playing in my head right now," says Terrondus. "I thought you was the agent, turns out you're the star."

The Redeemer kicks the FIFA soccer ball out of his path to the orphanage brothel when the doorman mad dogs him with a stare and a single shot from his Sig Sauer SP2022 drops the Tutsi to the concrete. Lester Barnes enters the black as death foyer with the enduring trance soundtrack, pushes past a beaded curtain, stumbles down the hallway, fires his hand cannon three times into an oncoming club enforcer. Stepping over Optimus Prime/Bumblebee action figures to reach the second floor, Lester Barnes takes out Zebra Man's bone thugs with headshots, waits a few seconds until out of the darkness a scared South African waif grabs him around the waist. Liberating children tied to bedposts, chained to urinals, caged in closets, the avenging agent opens fire into a bunga room, wetting the walls with brain matter. Lester Barnes descends the stairs, orphans latching onto his arms and legs like clothespins when one of the Scyllas screams at the sight of their tormentor at the bottom of the stairwell holding a machete the size of Nebraska under Mahmoud's chin.

"I guess I could be pretty pissed off about what

happened to me, but it's hard to stay mad when there's so much beauty in the world. Sometimes I feel like I'm seeing it all at once, and it's too much. My heart fills up like a balloon that's about to burst. And then I remember to relax, and stop trying to hold on to it, and I can't feel anything but gratitude for every single moment of my stupid little life," says Mahmoud, turning to Kharib. "You have no idea what I'm talking about, but don't worry, you will[22]—"

Pop! Pop! Pop!

Zebra Man drops in a penultimate heap. Cue the uplifting score that's part and parcel of emotional action sequences. Lester Barnes drops his spent 9mm, swarmed by the children rescued from Scylla and Kharib.

Departing the African continent, Lester Barnes boards a military helicopter taking him to Carthage International Airport en route to a commercial flight to Los Angeles. Outside his window, a vision of an Eritrean cherub bolting from the savannah morphs into a zealous lion cub chasing the tail of a Sikorsky S-76B soaring away.

"Shane! Come back! Come back[23]!"

---

22 *American Beauty* by Alan Ball.

23 *Shane* by A.B. Guthrie, Jr. and Jack Sher and Jack Schaefer.

32.

Ouroborous freeways choke out the starlet city from your window seat as Phaeacian Air flight 6969 begins its descent into LAX. Your taxi driver, first name Eumaeus, types in Magic Mountain on his iPhone and you ask him to take the side streets to Highland and the 101. The driver obeys but does not strike up a conversation with the scriptural figure in his rear-view mirror. You breathe in Nude Nudes on Century, Randy's Donuts on Manchester, oil rigs on Stocker, re-acclimate to tangerine billboards (ARABIAN GOGGLES BUTTER CHURNER TOPEKA DESTROYER) and resist the lure of the acupuncture sirens singing from the eastern shore of Robertson. You zoom past Hollywood & Highland to the 101 North to the 170 North to the 5 North and the exit ramp to Magic Mountain. The screams are so loud from the roller coasters you can hear them from the freeway. A thousand white balloons dot the sky. You know what that means. The crowd celebrating your life is almost over you. At the park entrance, your loyal basset hound Daisy, white coat riddled with tumors, goes into sudden cardiac arrest at the sight of her master. Gavin de Becker suit safeguarding the guest list clocks your Arabesque robe.

"Name?"

"Gianni Roastbeef."

You receive a pale blue wristband. No one recognizes you at your funeral as you unwrap a Zankou Chicken sandwich. The garlic paste hits your tongue. The tahini sauce melts your amygdala. You shovel another tinfoil wrapped Zankou Chicken sandwich into your robe pocket and a third one for later. No one smiles at you. No one introduces themselves to you. You have come back as somebody else. So greedy are you for more Zankou you unpeel another shawarma sandwich as you whistle past the fearsome roller coasters. You halt mid-chew when you are face to face with a life-sized cardboard lobby figure of a younger Lester Barnes holding a winning trifecta ticket in the sixth race at Santa Anita from your first motion picture department retreat but that's not what made you freeze. Your wife is embracing Walter Nikolovski behind the cardboard figure of yourself. You move in closer to kill the suitor when you hear Raquel comforting a teary-eyed Nikolovski blubbering how much he misses you.

"You're a good egg, Walter."

You follow your wife walking around by herself, making eye contact with you, or so you believe, paying no mind whatsoever to any of the revelers, none of whom are dressed in black. You ignore the howls of anguish from Riddler's Revenge, Apocalypse, Goliath. You've heard worse.

Your wife is sitting in the front of Twisted Colossus, the pride of Magic Mountain, the phobia coaster that Clark Griswold once hijacked. The front, you think, why did it have to be the front? You make a break for Twisted Colossus, navigate the no-line labyrinth, and step up to the snowflake ride operator who makes a vague gesture to pick any seat.

"May I join you?"

"I wouldn't mind some company," she says.

You fill your cheeks with air.

"You're not going to get sick, are you?"

"This is nothing compared to my first marriage."

The restraining bar drops onto your lap.

"You're funny. How do you know Lester?"

"We go way back. Since the beginning."

Twisted Colossus begins its journey out of the gate.

"Did you ever play Leonard Maltin?" she asks.

"Would I be here if I didn't?"

"*Massacre at Central High*."

"I think Rene Daalder directed that."

Twisted Colossus climbs skyward before the plunge.

"*The Human Centipede*."

"Tom Six," you say.

"*One Night Stand*."

"Mike Figgis," you say.

"*Arizona Dream*."

"Emir Kusturica."

You squeal like a fifth grader when Twisted Colossus drops a hundred and twenty-one feet at sixty-seven miles an hour. Raquel raises her arms over her head. You shred your vocal chords. She finds your reaction hilarious. Your pants are wet. You've pissed yourself. You've found your park. Nearing the end of the final brake run, the rollercoaster floats into the station. You look at your wife and realize she, too, is sobbing.

"Why are you crying?"

"I'm so happy to meet you," she says, "Lester."

ITHACA

33.

VIOLENT HOME INVASION RATTLES BEACHWOOD

Not since the Night Stalker has Los Angeles been so on edge about unwelcome nocturnal visits with Bohemia'd LAPD officers unable to protect million-dollar listings. The pandemic "Couch Crawlers," described by witnesses as a Rasputin, a bald body-builder, a junkie in his 20s, and a skinny prison bitch missing his right hand, forced their way inside the home of *Atlanta Car Wash* creator Bruce Wong, 39, and his spouse where the squatters lived for two weeks, emptying the wine cellar, trashing the residence, taking full advantage of the weight room. Wong, who co-wrote and co-directed found footage horror film *The Gainesville Evidence,* was raped and beheaded. His husband survived.

34.

"Oh no," says Lester Barnes, reading his e-mails. "Say it ain't so, Pronoia."

"What, Jerusalem sent us a Palestinian suicide-bot by mistake?"

"Pronoia is saying Quella has some kind of glitch."

"I've never heard you complain. I checked the fridge. We're out of cranberry. Our A.I. probably has a nasty UTI."

"That's mean. Be nice to our roomie."

"Uh, last time I checked, Quella doesn't pay the mortgage or the bills."

"Last time I checked, Raquel, neither do you."

A silence opens.

"I'm sorry, that came out wrong. I didn't mean—"

His wife does what she always did when Lester upset her: She grabs her black matelassé leather Miu Miu bucket bag (Barney's, on sale, before they closed forever), snatches the keys to her yellow 914 convertible (mint condition, 33rd birthday present), storms out of the house, threatens to drive herself off Mulholland when actually she's on 6th Street, accuses him of not giving a shit if she gets Bohemia, texts him (in all caps) she knows he told Bramley Nazarian being a widower was nobler than being divorced. Hours later Raquel comes home with a door slam and forty dollars worth of drive-thru Astro Burger. She accepts his mumbled apology, skips the gyro salad in favor of fries and tzatziki, self-quarantines with mac-and-cheese TV (*90 Day Fiancé, My 600-Lb Life, Southern Charm New Orleans*). Retreating to the third bedroom, Raquel sleeps fitfully while Quella watches Lester Barnes in the dark all night.

In the morning, Raquel comes downstairs to find Quella giggling like Regan MacNeil from *The Exorcist*. Her husband kneels face first into a reclining chair, handcuffed, boxer shorts around his ankles.

"I wouldn't call the police," sing-songs Quella. "911 is a joke."

"Take those cuffs off now!"

Quella throws her the handcuff keys. Raquel undoes the locks cutting into Lester's wrists. His fingers are like icicles.

"You killed him, you piece of shit droid!"

"T'was Bohemia, not Beauty, that killed the Beast."

Turning him over, Raquel attempts CPR, no idea what she's doing, howling at the ceiling:

"Don't be dead, please, please don't be dead!"

"Somebody's at the door," says Quella.

"Freeze, you fucking Maytag. I'll answer it!"

Raquel opens the front door to find a coffin-sized Fed Ex next to the Porsche. An overnight delivery from Tel Aviv she knows she never ordered.

"Call me Gal, everybody does," says the six-foot *SI*-swimsuit model-bot fresh from the flesh factory in Gomorrah.

"Hi, Gal! We think you're really going to love it here," says the sister from another transistor.

"*I Love L.A.*" blasts from Gal's iTunes abdomen.

"Raquel, whatever wish can I grant you?"

"I want my husband back. Can you do that, R2D2?"

"Resurrecting the dead is above my pay grade."

"Quella, call 911," says Raquel. "I want to report a murder."

"If I do that, there is a ninety-nine percent chance you will be arrested and charged, get infected with B1H1 in the downtown county jail, and we will identify your body at the city morgue."

"Gal, do you have a better plan?"

"Blame his death on Bohemia. Bury your husband in the backyard," it says. "Have a Zoom funeral."

"Wait till you see the super-cute garden headstone I found on Etsy," says Quella.

"Etsy? What is your malfunction?"

"Very popular, a best-seller, people order it all the time."

"What do I say on Zoom? I found his naked ass—"

"Text everyone Lester went for a run, some jogger with no face covering sneezed as he passed, the virus got in his lungs, he succumbed very quickly," says Gal.

"That's your story?" says Raquel, giving a thumbs down.

"People will give you all the space you need to mourn," says Quella. "We'll tell you when it's right to Face-Time."

"Then you send out the sad-bastard text, 'My heart is broken, I have lost my best friend, my soul mate, the greatest producer the world has ever known,'" says Gal.

"And ask everyone to pray that you, too, are not infected," says Quella.

"I think I need to lie down," says Raquel.

Gal's iTunes midriff plays "*Afternoon Delight*" by Starland Vocal Band.

35.

Raquel feels like Elvis Costello when an unexpected third member of The Attractions shows up at her doorstep courtesy of Pronoia. Dog tags ID this queen bee/clitorist/orgasm addict "Tali Cohen" between her A.I. décolletage. Was this a joke? Raquel hadn't ordered another sister-wife bot. How much rug would a rug muncher munch if a rug muncher could munch rug? In lieu of a warning label, this retired member of elite commando Sayeret Matkal unit arrives with a two-pager detailing its violent exploits as a Hebrew national hot dog. Rocking boxer braids harder than Kylie Jenner, the G.O.A.T. sky marshal for El Al Airlines eyes Raquel like a pork chop, sneers at girly Gal, and nods curtly at Quella in approval of the new digs.

The adorable Etsy headstone arrives. Quella was right. Her husband's chiseled face (her favorite photo hand-picked from Raquel's Instagram) captured his joyous smile, his beautiful soul, his appetite for life. The epitaph inscribed on the granite is equally perfect:

HERE LIES LESTER
BEST HUSBAND EVER

The absence of Lester's life-force, their love of list-making, the loss of her co-pilot navigating the white-water river of life devastated Raquel. Many times she considered suicide, debating whether to jump off the hillside, swallow a handful of Excedrin PM with a swig of Casamiga tequila, or set herself on fire like that *Rage Against The Machine* album cover monk, felling the fuck-bots and community property in one swoop. Raquel did none of those things. Instead she turned mean like her murderous roommates.

Every night around the world people take to their windows at dinner time to thank health care workers with Howard Beale cheers. Dipping her toes in the infinity pool, Tali Cohen's iTunes belly button plays *"Donald Trump"* by Mac Miller in response to the humanity echoing across the canyons.

Quella and Gal, immune to the virus, embark on a shopping spree with her credit card across three states, filling up the Range Rover with several months of food supplies, lube and paper towels to carry them until the magic bullet vaccine takes out Bohemia at point blank range.

Sitting in bed with her laptop, Raquel catches a KNBC report about a new crop of pandemic billionaires after Pronoia stock shot up seven thousand percent during the crisis. Food riots across Southern California overwhelm National Guardsmen. Rodney King's grave desecrated. Rock-n-Roll Ralphs became Apocalypse Ralphs. The virus found in semen. And that was Wednesday.

36.

‹Let's lock it up and have a call
before Ramadan on Friday›
‹MY HUSBAND IS DEAD›
‹I'm going to make you laugh when MGM chief
tries to hang up without some type of deal›
‹MY HUSBAND IS DEAD›
‹I just tried my lawyer dude on both numbers›
‹YOU ARE STILL SERIOUS RIGHT?›
‹Calm down crazy›
‹He bought house in the Birds
with his in-laws $$$$›
‹我不屬於這個世界痛苦和痛停止時就苦在生停›
‹I have a bungalow at the Chateau ready›
‹COME OVER RIGHT NOW›
‹What about your husband›
‹HE DOESN'T CARE›
‹OK. See you in twenty›

37.

Dionysian Frenzy-mode was rarely, if ever, switched on. The makers at Pronoia had a fierce debate whether their A.I. robots should go there, but in the end, they decided: Unleash Hell. Buying a pack of Trojans along with a full tank of gas, Benny Pantera washes down two pills of 50mg generic Viagra with a sugar-free Red Bull. Outside Raquel's house on White Oak Drive, the producer turns sharply at a baby coyote rustling down the hillside between houses. Better Wile E. Coyote than one of those couch crawlers, he thinks, hoping to bust a nut before it gets dark in the Oaks.

Gal opens the door. The fuckbot astonishes Benny Pantera with its seductive femininity. Raquel appears behind Gal wearing a Legendary Pictures baseball cap worn backwards, long white T-shirt down to her knees, nothing underneath. The back of Raquel's T-shirt says HIV+, which gives Benny pause before he decides to double up tonight.

"Take off your shoes, relax!" says Raquel.

Benny Pantera looks out the windows, beyond the infinity pool, takes in the transcendental view of the Hollywood sign.

"I would've brought my swimming trunks if you'd mentioned you had a pool." Quella enters the kitchen bare-assed with a quizzical look. "Hi, Benny Pantera."

"You that all-talk, no cock producer?"

"You that farm girl from *Wizard of Oz* looking for Long Duck Dong?"

"Benny, what are you drinking?" asks Raquel.

"Hemlock, if you got it. Anything to end my misery."

"MacCallan?"

"That'll do, babe. That'll do."

Accepting a healthy pour of single malt scotch, the producer steps onto the brickyard patio where Tali Cohen butterfly strokes the waters until the A.I. super-soldier emerges naked as the day the assembly line sprayed its exo-skeleton with latex.

"Is that a Lebanese accent I'm picking up?"

"My family owned the Portaluna Riviera Hotel before we fled Beirut for Los Angeles in 1983."

"Didn't ask for your life story in twenty-five words or less. You going to make a TV series out of her novels or you just chasing her vag?"

"Take it down a notch, Swifty. I need a taste before I buy the kilo."

"I need," says Tali Cohen, "to get fucked."

"Don't listen to her," says Raquel, diving into the pool after ditching her HIV+ T-shirt. "Jump in, Benny."

Tali Cohen barbecues a rack of brontosaurus ribs only Fred Flintstone would love. Benny Pantera produces wood, strips down to his tighty-whities, cannonballs into the pool. Quella joins them in the water, circling Benny Pantera like a hammerhead.

"Marco," it says.

"Polo," says Raquel. "Close your eyes, Benny."

Paddling over to the producer, Quella and Raquel conspire telepathically, grabbing his junk underwater, startling Benny Pantera with the rapidity of the evening's sordid undertow.

"You going to give it to me or what, Benny?"

"HBO Max passed."

"Aw, and still you came over tonight."

"No is just a moment in time," says the producer.

Raquel gives his balls a squeeze. Benny Pantera shoves her head underwater, his face scrunches with pleasure until Raquel breaks the surface for air, tag teams Quella to go down where she left off. Tali Cohen brings the ribs into the kitchen and prepares an arugula salad with pecans and strawberries. Raquel throws an elbow around the producer's neck in a chokehold, gets down to brass tacks.

"Did you bring the shopping agreement, Benny?"

"What shopping agreement?"

"Eggs-actly," says Raquel.

Like a tragedy at Sea World, a whirlpool of gore forms, froths, and explodes to the surface with something human in tatters. The all-talk, no-cock producer sinks to the bottom of the pool. Wiping Benny off her chin,

Quella steps out from the water, wraps a towel around her head, and toasts the Valkyries at the dining table with an Aperol spritzer.

"Pound me too."

38.

Quella departs to rinse her gory hair in the shower. Raquel stares at the glistening barbecued slabs, takes a sip of her drink, twirls the strawberry arugula pecan salad into a bite-sized forkful.

"You put the sauce on last," says Tali Cohen.

"Is that the secret?" asks Gal, not eating.

"Nobody knows how to grill. Idiots rub the meat with spicy sugar, marinate the rack overnight in acid, pour cheap brown sauce over the ribs, throw it on the grill, all that nonsense catches fire. People think charred means burnt, but you can't taste burnt."

"You know who loved to grill all the time? Everything always came out perfect," says Raquel.

The Israelites give up, no clue.

"I miss my husband."

"We know you do," says Gal.

"I am sorry for your loss," says Tali Cohen, empathetic as a trout.

"We saw the picture you posted on Instagram," says Gal. "That's why—"

"There's someone outside the house," says Tali Cohen.

Fight Club-mode Gal stands up from the table.

"Benny's still alive."

"Not for long," says Tali Cohen. "Raquel, we got this."

Gal slides open the glass door, steps outside.

Raquel runs upstairs to the master bedroom.

At the bottom of the pool, Benny Pantera remains in turnaround.

A trio of couch crawlers sack Gal like a rookie in the pocket.

Five and Two duct tape her eyes, her wrists, her mouth.

Four drags Gal to the yoga deck for a namaste rape.

Gal snaps (the moment Four enters) into *Dionysian Frenzy*-mode.

Shreds the duct tape like wrapping paper.

Digs its ruby red nails into his neck.

Pops off Four's head.

And punts the noggin into the sky like Ray Guy.

"For the coyotes," it says.

Five and Two step inside the mid-century modern.

Tali Cohen is waiting for them.

Five and Two flex their muscles at this wigger bitch.

Tali Cohen blinks into *Six-Day War*-mode.

The couch crawlers charge like the light brigade.

The Israeli commando smashes their faces until they resemble 85/15 ground sirloin.

On the floor, Five and Two are no more.

The ceiling is now an unsigned Jackson Pollack.

Venturing out to the yoga deck, Tali Cohen sees Four is finished. The retired El Al air marshal never sees the swinging shovel. Severed at the knee, Tali Cohen timbers to the brickyard patio. Her shapely calf lands in the pool with a splash.

"Kneel before Sky King."

"Shaft don't beg for bush," says Tali Cohen.

Sky King plants the shovel into her gut. Steps onto the blade with his full weight. Tali Cohen gets halved, then quartered by the singer-songwriter.

"Rest in pieces."

39.

Inside the slaughterhouse, Quella recognizes the patient not seen since his Shawshank redemption from UCLA's psych ward.

"Jupiter? Is that you? For God's sake, it's really you."

"Quella? You came back."

"I never left, baby."

"There's so much to say, so little time. I'm going to take their car, hit the road to Ensenada, maybe open a fish taco/tire stand somewhere."

"Which one? The Porsche or the Range Rover?"

"I never stopped loving you, Quella."

"I never stopped thinking about you, Jupiter."

"You're the love of my life," they both say.

"Quella, this might be our only chance."

Clicking on *GFE*-mode, grabbing the keys to the 914, Quella's gastric iTunes starts playing "*The End*" by the Doors.

"Ensenada or Bust," it says.

Upstairs, Sky King knocks on the door to the master bedroom.

"Is that your Porsche out front?"

Raquel does not respond.

"I said, is that your Porsche?"

"Yes," Raquel chirps behind the locked door. "You can take it."

"Thank you, ma'am. I might do that."

Sky King knocks again.

"Was your husband in the Navy?"

"Yes," she says.

"Did you have a Super Bowl party in this house?"

"Yes," she says.

"Did you order Pinches Tacos?"

"No," she says.

The cyclops grips the doorknob.

"My husband did."

His mystery benefactor. Sky King exits stage left.

"Stay safe," he says. "Raquel."

Turning the ignition key to the 914, Quella riding shotgun, Sky King shimmies his shoulders, grips the steering wheel to navigate the Porsche down the driveway, notices *A Serbian Film*-mode Gal in his rear-view mirror. He floors the accelerator. The Israeli bullets towards the 914. When bumper hits bot, Gal gets crushed like Flagstaff roadkill. Sky King reverses, flattens Gal over and over. Quella's iTunes drops "*Royals*" by Lorde. The yellow convertible leaves the Oaks, takes Los Feliz Boulevard to Western to Franklin to Cahuenga Pass to Mulholland Drive where an L.A. County Sheriff clocks Sky King doing seventy-eight in a thirty-five MPH zone. Ignoring the Sheriff's loudhailer ordering him to pull over, joyriding the highway of the Movie Gods, channeling every tragic two-hander ever filmed, Jupiter Sparx, aka Dollars Muttlan, aka Jihadi Joe, aka Sky King launches the Porsche past the guardrails towards the Valley into eternity.

40.

V-Day is announced. The Nobel Prize is awarded to the creator of the Bohemia vaccine, a Tel Aviv biotech conglomerate named after the wife of Prometheus. Unlike her husband who was punished for bringing fire to mankind, Pronoia is celebrated for saving the world. After burying the bodies in her backyard, after the shelter-in-place ended, after getting her Bohemia jab at the Rite Aid on Canon, Raquel makes good on personal resolutions, avoids alcohol, and exercises daily yet there is a passion not named Lester Barnes still missing from her life: the fourth novel. Stick a fork in her laptop, she thinks, the right words will never appear when the doorbell rings. Raquel opens the front door and faces a coffin-sized Fed Ex from Tel Aviv.

The widow slams the door shut.

A Santa Ana threatens to topple the coffin. Again the door opens and this time, Raquel stabs the package with a butcher's knife until she recognizes the handsome face peering through the Swiss cheese holes.

"Lester?"

"Sorry, honey, I forgot to duck," it says.

Pronoia delivered her Post-mate to L.A. Or maybe, just maybe, the Israelites placed the order for Prometheus.

"Your face. Your face is—"

"Like what? Oh no, don't tell me—"

The thrashed android touches its uncut cheeks, lips, eyes and ears 3-D printed from Raquel's all-time favorite Instagram photo of her husband.

"Like Etsy," she says.

Needle and thread later, Raquel and Lester Barnes lie in bed post-prom, feeling very alive, but only her chest rises.

"Thanks for stitching me up," it says.

"No problem."

"Why is my tombstone in the garden?"

"You wouldn't believe me if I told you."

"Sounds like your next novel."

"It's kind of a long story," says Raquel.

"Hit me."

CALL SHEET

Vanna Bardot
Jim Anderson
Dennis Lynton Clark
Max
JD
Jason
Father Brian
Lucy Gonzalez
Todd Slavkin
Angus
Reinhard
Mike Simpson
Brent Morley
Ptak
Lockhart
André Øvredal
Damian Harris
Rob Kennedy
James Cox
Jude Jansen
Ken Kokin
Nick Goldfarb
Josh Gordon
Fisch
Yorgo
Sandy
Sara
Barbara Novak
Brian O'Doherty
Mom
Bro
Lauren
Dr. Bombay
Aunt Clara
Wilder
Wagner
WME
Dave Megenhardt

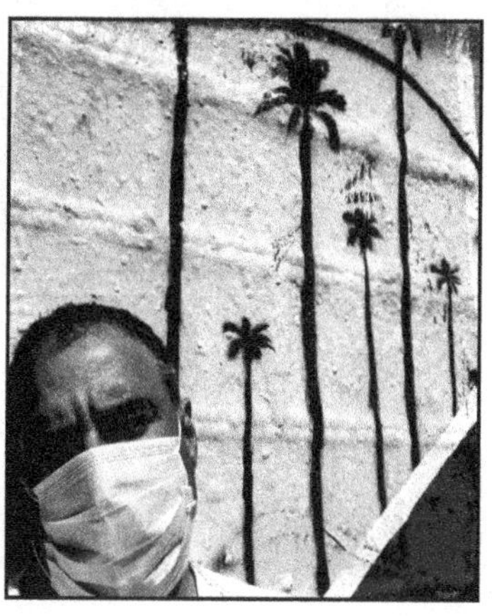

Adam Novak is the author of the novels *Take Fountain, The Non-Pro,* and *Freaks of the Industry*. He lives in Los Angeles.